T0246174

FAITH'S ANSWERS
— *to* —
AMERICA'S POLITICAL CRISIS

FAITH'S ANSWERS

— *to* —

AMERICA'S POLITICAL CRISIS

---

*How Religion Can Help Us
Out of the Mess We're In*

S E N A T O R
JOE LIEBERMAN

A POST HILL PRESS BOOK
ISBN: 979-8-88845-303-2
ISBN (eBook): 979-8-88845-304-9

Cover design by Cody Corcoran

This is a work of nonfiction. All people, locations, events, and situations are portrayed to the best of the author's memory.

Post Hill Press
New York • Nashville
posthillpress.com

Published in the United States of America
1 2 3 4 5 6 7 8 9 10

CONTENTS

Introduction...ix

Chapter One: It All Begins with God 1

Chapter Two: Partisanship... 17

Chapter Three: Political and Governmental Reform Will Not
        Happen Without Strong Leaders............................. 29

Chapter Four: Incivility.. 43

Chapter Five: Distrust 55

Chapter Six: The Demise of Debate 71

Chapter Seven: The Unwillingness to Compromise 83

Chapter Eight: Do We Really Need Governments?................ 95

Chapter Nine: Have the Partisanship and Division in
        Our Politics and Government Mattered to Our
        Legal System? 107

Chapter Ten: Does the Partisanship in Our Politics Affect
        America's Security in the World? 117

Chapter Eleven: America Needs a Religious Awakening and a
        New Political Covenant.. 131

INTRODUCTION

Every time I took an oath of office—to be state senator, attorney general, or US senator—I put one hand on a bible and concluded my oath with the words "so help me God." That was a powerful, personal reminder that the basis of my public service, and that of everyone else who has taken that same oath, was faith in God.

Can the faith in God that the great majority of Americans share help us out of the political mess we're in? That is the question I will try to answer in this book.

Our country is divided and pessimistic, our people are insecure and angry, our government is less functional and trustworthy, and our politics are nastier and more partisan than they have been for a long time...maybe ever. Everything we have done thus far to try to reunite America and make our government work again hasn't worked. Maybe it's time to bring God's values back into America's public life.

We need to see if faith in God can help us meet our most serious domestic and international challenges. If we pray about it, think about it, and, most important, bring our behavior in line with the lessons our shared faith in

God teaches us, can we restore national unity, solve our biggest domestic problems, and overcome our international challenges?

I believe we can.

That is the case I will make in this book—that our shared belief in God can help us solve our most difficult societal, political, and international problems. I will direct my argument to the 535 members of Congress, the president, and his staff; the people who control our news, entertainment entities, and social media platforms; and the leaders of our churches, synagogues, and mosques, because they are the ones who are most capable of turning our country around, and of leading a national religious awakening that can lead to transformational political reforms.

Politicians and the media that cover them need to pull themselves back from the daily political crossfire and feverish quest for more campaign money, more votes, bigger audiences, and bigger profits. They need to return to our shared national values, based on the Judeo-Christian tradition that has been called America's civil religion. It is a religion that is deist, open, and inclusive and should be at the heart of our public life, but it certainly is not now.

Religious leaders need to teach their followers about how the principles of our faith in God can and should unite us and raise our government up again. They might also challenge their congregants to ask themselves whether they have begun to make earthly idols out of their political party or ideology, or out of the cable news channels and the social media they frequent.

In meeting this challenge, clergy can find some encouraging data: God still has many more supporters in our country than any American political leader—living or dead—and much more than any political party today. More than 90 percent of the American people say they believe in a "higher power," and more than 80 percent say they believe in the one God of the three major monotheistic Abrahamic faiths, according to a Pew Research Center survey published in December 2017.

That matters because if you are Christian, Jewish, or Muslim, you are in the majority of the 330 million citizens of America and, for that matter, the eight billion people on Earth. According to the latest estimates, there are 2.4 billion Christians and 1.8 billion Muslims in the world. The third-largest religion is Hinduism, with 1.2 billion members. While Hinduism has many gods and goddesses, they are all seen by most Hindus as the embodiment of the divine Brahman, who is God. A 2021 Pew Research Center poll of Hindus in India found that 97 percent believed in God. I therefore view Hinduism as another monotheistic faith, different in origin from the Abrahamic faiths but tied to them by a shared belief in God.

There is not currently much evidence that a significant number of American monotheists see that their belief in the one God who created Heaven and Earth should lead them naturally to different behavior in government and politics than is most common today. If we can convince them to apply the principles of their faith to public issues and behavior, that would surely help repair our country and the world.

Let me focus, as an example, on one bedrock tenet of the three major monotheistic faiths and what it teaches us. Believing in one God who created each of us means that we are all children of the same Father—sisters and brothers. It also means that each of us is created in the image of God, with a spark of our divine Creator in us, and all of us therefore deserve to be treated equally with respect and kindness. In his essay "The Genesis of Justice," Lord Jonathan Sacks, the late chief rabbi of the United Kingdom, described this belief as "perhaps the most transformative in the entire history of moral and political thought. It is the basis of the civilization of the west with its unique emphasis on the individual and on equality. It lies behind Thomas Jefferson's words in the American Declaration of Independence, '...that all men are created equal [and] are endowed by their Creator with certain inalienable rights.'"

And this tenet is at the heart of the competition we are engaged in with officially atheist states such as China and North Korea, and totalitarian inhumane regimes such as Iran and Russia.

Applying foundational monotheistic beliefs to America's current political crisis can lead our elected leaders to treat each other with the respect we owe each other as fellow creations of God. It should guide our leaders in Washington to have civil discussions about our problems and our disagreements, to listen respectfully to each other's differing views, and to work together to compromise and collaborate to find common ground to solve them. That would end the prevailing, automatic partisan and ideological mudslinging in which members of one party seem to view members of other parties not just as wrong on policy but as evil, and definitely not as sisters and brothers. They treat each other uncivilly, refuse to listen to each other, and rarely compromise for the common good.

America needs a New American Political Covenant and a Twenty-First-Century Religious Awakening to bring people back to these truths. It would be like the religious awakenings in the eighteenth century that enabled the American Revolution and independence, and those in the nineteenth and twentieth centuries that empowered America to end slavery, repeal legal segregation, enact laws to lessen the suffering of poor people, curb social injustices, and win two world wars and a cold war. I will describe such a covenant and such an awakening in the concluding chapter.

Belief in God is a proven motivator for moral behavior and social justice. Our first president, George Washington, understood that and declared in his memorable Farewell Address in 1796:

> Of all the dispositions and habits which
> lead to political prosperity, religion and

morality are indispensable supports....
Let us with caution indulge the suppo-
sition that morality can be maintained
without religion.

On the other hand, we all also know agnostics and athe-
ists who are moral people working to make our country and
world better. So, religion is not the only guarantor of morality, but it is probably the best.

I write this book as someone who believes in God and
tries to live within the values and traditions of my Jewish
religion. That is the faith tradition that I know best and will
therefore cite most often, but I will also try to describe the
fundamental beliefs, values, and aspirations that the three
monotheistic Abrahamic faiths and other religions, including Hinduism, share that can help us all overcome our political divisions and growing hopelessness.

I am not a clergyman or a theologian. I was trained as
a lawyer and have spent most of my life in public service.
However, I have also spent a lot of time studying and think-
ing about the role of religion in America's public life and in
my personal life. And I have written two books on religious
subjects: one called *The Gift of Rest*, about the beauty of the
Sabbath, and the other called *With Liberty and Justice*, about
the impact God's giving of the Ten Commandments had on
our legal system and our societal values. In this current book,
I will argue that the two worlds in which I have lived—one

political and public, the other religious and private—need to be brought together in America's public square now to help our beloved and besieged country become a better, stronger place at home and abroad.

CHAPTER ONE

It All Begins with God

Belief in one God is the foundation for all the lessons we Americans can possibly learn from our faith to help us raise up our politics and government. Anyone who believes in the one God who created Heaven, Earth, and people must also believe that all humans are tied together as children of the same Creator and that all are equal with one another from birth. In the Talmud, the compilation of Jewish law and ethics, it is written: "Whoever saves one life, it is as if he saved the entire world" (Mishna Sanhedrin 4:5).

The Talmud derives this provocative conclusion from the Bible. God began the human race by creating one man, Adam, and then one woman, Eve, and from them came the rest of human history. If the life of Adam had ended before Eve was created, that would also have been the end of the human race. And so, we believe that in every person there is the future potential of the entire world, as there was with

Adam and Eve. The Talmud wisely adds that human history began with God's creation of one person "for the sake of peace among human beings so that a man should not say to his fellow 'My father is greater than your father.'" (Sanhedrin 37a:11–14) And I would update that to say, so a politician should never say to a member of another party, "My party is greater than your party and therefore I am greater than you."

We have the same Father, and that means we owe each other respect, regardless of the ways in which we may be different from one another. Our shared paternity is what should be most important in our personal, communal, and political lives. It is the premise of every democracy in the world, including ours, as the great Committee of Five wrote in America's Declaration of Independence detailing our separation from Great Britain in 1776. The following words they wrote are some of the most important ever written in the English language:

> We hold these truths to be self-evident,
> that all men are created equal, that they
> are endowed by their Creator with certain
> inalienable rights that among these are
> life, liberty and the pursuit of happiness.

It was to secure these rights, as the Declaration says in the very next sentence, that our country's founders were ready to fight England for their independence. Their great initiative began a new democratic chapter in the way people would govern themselves throughout the world. And it all began with God and those "inalienable rights."

Belief in God, the Creator, also means we do not think we exist as an accident of nature. Instead, we are alive as a result of an intentional decision by God to create the world and all that is in it, including us humans. All major religions have that fundamental belief, and therefore all people of faith have reason to feel good about themselves. We exist as the result of an intentional act of God that was carried out, according to every deist faith, with love and kindness. That, in turn, should reinforce our responsibility to live according to God's laws and values, and give us the confidence to believe we can.

The same is true for Hindus who believe in Brahma as the God of Creation, and that every person has a soul that is Brahman, because it comes from that supreme force present in all things.

Judaism, Christianity, and Islam share not only faith in God but faith in our biblical "parents"—Abraham, Isaac, Jacob, and Moses—uniting us in both faith and family. God's covenant with Abraham and, through him, with all humans, was the beginning of monotheism. In Hebrew, the name Abraham means "father of nations," and that is what Abraham became. As the Bible tells us, Abraham rebelled against the idol worshippers in his family and community, and destroyed his father's idols. When God saw that Abraham was loyal to Him, He made a covenant with him and called on him to leave his family and country and go to the land that God promised him. The Bible tells us that later, when God decided to destroy the sinful people of Sodom and Gomorrah, He said, "Shall I hide from Abraham what I am about to do?... For I have chosen him, that he may command his children and his household after him to keep the way of the Lord by doing righteousness and justice" (Genesis 18:17–19 ESV).

It is miraculous that today, Abraham's monotheistic descendants constitute a majority of the people on Earth. It is miraculous because it all began with a covenant between God and one man. We who are Abraham's descendants have a responsibility to remember God's confidence that we would keep that "way of God doing charity and justice." We should be faithful to God's values and live by God's laws in every aspect of our lives, including politics.

Abraham's grandson, Jacob, had a son, Joseph, who was sold into slavery by his jealous brothers and brought to Egypt, the superpower of that time. In another miracle, Joseph quickly went from slavery and prison to becoming the second-most powerful person in Egypt. When famine struck Canaan, the land that God had promised Abraham and his descendants, Jacob and his children moved to Egypt for food and survival, and eventually lived very well under Joseph's rule. But then Joseph and the pharaoh who had promoted him died, and another man, who did not know Joseph, became the pharaoh. The new ruler enslaved all the Israelites, because they had grown from a small family to a very big—and, to the new pharaoh, threatening—tribe. The Israelites suffered terribly in slavery until God heard their cries and remembered His covenant with Abraham. He sent Moses, whose heart He found as faithful as He had Abraham's, to lead them out of bondage. When Moses appealed to the pharaoh on behalf of God to "let my people go," he added the words "to serve God." Moses' mission was not to liberate the Israelites from slavery into Egyptian society, where they probably would have assimilated and disappeared, or for them to wander lawlessly and aimlessly in the desert outside Egypt, where they probably would have destroyed each other. Instead, Moses, at God's direction, was to lead the Israelites to Mount Sinai, where God would give them and the world the Ten Commandments, a system of law to govern themselves—and subsequently, ourselves.

In the first two of the Ten Commandments, God declares that He is the God who brought them out of Egypt, and that we should have no other gods before Him. In those sentences, God ordains monotheism and establishes the strongest possible basis for the legal code that He promulgates in the remaining eight commandments. They come from God. There were legal systems before Sinai, but none of them began with one God—the Creator and Redeemer.

Christianity and Islam embrace much of the historical narrative of the Hebrew Bible, including the Ten Commandments.

In the Gospel of Matthew 19:16–19, it is written:

> And, behold, one came and said unto
> him [that is, Matthew], Good Master,
> what good thing shall I do, that I may
> have eternal life?
>
> And he said unto him, Why callest thou
> me good? There is none good but one,
> that is, God: but if thou wilt enter into
> life, keep the commandments.
>
> He saith unto him, Which? Jesus said,
> Thou shalt do no murder, Thou shalt not
> commit adultery, Thou shalt not steal,
> Thou shalt not bear false witness,
>
> Honour thy father and thy mother: and,
> Thou shalt love thy neighbour as thyself.
> (KJV)

The *Catechism of the Catholic Church* (Chapter 3, Article 1, Section III) puts Jesus' embrace of the Ten Commandments into a theological and historical context:

> The Lord's sermon on the mount, far
> from abolishing or devaluing the moral
> principles of the Old Law releases their
> hidden potential...[and] reveals their
> entire Divine and human truth.

Faith's Answers to America's Political Crisis

Islam began in the seventh century when the Prophet Muhammad declared in the words of the Quran what God had revealed to him. The Quran embraces both the Hebrew Torah and the Christian gospels:

> He has revealed to you, O Prophet, the Book in truth, confirming what came before it as He revealed the Torah and the Gospel previously, as a guide for people...to distinguish between right and wrong. (Surah 3:3–4)

It is remarkable that after the Prophet, the two people mentioned most often in the Quran are Moses and Jesus. Although Hinduism, the largest non-Abrahamic religious faith, does not follow the Ten Commandments of the Abrahamic faiths, at its center are ethical values and guidelines that flow from its faith in Brahma, the Creator and Sustainer. Sage Patanjali's Yoga Sutras offer ten principles of thought and behavior that are found in Hindu scripture and teachings. Five are called *yamas* and should be the basis for thoughts and actions: compassion, truth, respect for others' property, moderation, and avoidance of greed. The other five are called *niyamas* and are guides for every believer's personal behavior: cleanliness, contentment, self-discipline, self-reflection, and surrender to Brahman, the ultimate divine reality.

This theological and textual history, which will surprise most people, shows how intertwined Judaism, Christianity, and Islam have been from their beginnings, and how similar Hinduism is to them. Jesus was a Jewish rabbi who believed in the Torah and its values. Muhammad heard the word of God, which was recorded in the Quran and built on the spiritual foundations and texts of Judaism and Christianity that were around Muhammad in Arabia.

Although religion has too often since then been a terrible divider and cause of human suffering among people, the shared history and beliefs of the beginnings of the major monotheistic faiths should remind us of how much we share, and hopefully bring us closer together.

The Quran (Surah Araf 7:142–145) describes the meeting of Moses with God on Mount Sinai to receive the Ten Commandments in these words:

> And we wrote for him, Moses on the Tablets, the lesson to be drawn from all things…. Hold on to these with firmness.

The Quran also records the story of Moses breaking the tablets he had brought down from Sinai after he saw the Israelites worshipping an idol they had made in his absence. In Surah 7:154 it then says:

> And when the anger of Musa was appeased, he took up the Tablets, and in

their inscription was guidance and mercy
for those who fear the Lord.

Later in the Quran (Taqi-ud-Din Hilali 6:151–153) it is
written in the name of Muhammad:

> And verily this [the Ten Command-
> ments as enumerated in the Quran] is
> my straight path, so follow it and follow
> not other paths, for they will separate
> you away from His path. This He has
> ordained for you that you may become
> the [pious].

Even when divisions have emerged among or within
the major monotheistic faiths, the common understanding
of where we all came from and how we should therefore
behave has remained strong. Just as Christianity argues that
Jesus came not to deny the Torah but to improve it, Muhammad declared that Islam was a reformation, not a rejec-
tion of Judaism and Christianity. In Christianity, during the
sixteenth century, reformers did reject some of the theology
and practices of the Roman Catholic Church. However,
there remained much faith and practice that these Protestants shared with Catholics and with the other monotheistic
religions. The Protestants gave the Hebrew Bible and its laws
a central place in their theology. They explicitly held that the
Ten Commandments Moses received from God on Mount

Sinai were a clear expression of Christian moral values. The Church of England declared in the Thirty-Nine Articles of Religion that "no Christian...is free from the obedience to the Commandments which are called moral."

The deepening of divisions among Christians in England eventually led the first Pilgrims from there to America. Most of them were Calvinists who argued for separation from the Church of England because they viewed the Church as corrupted by its involvement in politics and by materialism. The Pilgrims decided they had no choice but to leave England to find religious freedom, first briefly settling in Holland and then sailing on the *Mayflower* to America. When their ship landed at Plymouth, Massachusetts, in November 1620, their spiritual leader, William Brewster, led them onto Plymouth Rock and sang King David's Psalm 100, which is full of gratitude to God:

> Make a joyful noise unto the LORD, all ye lands. Serve the LORD with gladness: Come before His presence with singing. Know ye that the LORD He is God: It is He that hath made us, and not we ourselves; We are His people, and the sheep of His pasture. Enter into His gates with thanksgiving, And into His courts with praise: Be thankful unto Him, and bless His name. For the LORD is good; His

mercy is everlasting; And His truth en-
dureth to all generations. (KJV)

Those were the first words of the first English Pilgrim
to step onto American land. His descendants created the
United States of America a century and a half later.

It could be said that these words of King David sung by
the Calvinist William Brewster in the first minutes of our
nation's history began America's Judeo-Christian tradition.

The men who emerged in the eighteenth century as
leaders of the American Revolution and eventually the new
American government were all believers in that religious
and ethical tradition. As Michael Novak, the late Roman
Catholic theologian and historian, wrote in his book *On
Two Wings*, the American government was able to take off
because it had two strong but different wings. One was the
philosophy of the Enlightenment in Europe. The other,
often overlooked or undervalued by historians, was the
Calvinist Christian faith of our Founding Fathers, which
centered on a belief in the Bible and in the one God, the
Creator and Redeemer.

Our Founding Fathers believed that God, not government, was the source of human rights and the rule of law,
going back to Creation and the Ten Commandments given
on Sinai.

This theology underlaid and energized the American
Revolution and was the rock on which the revolutionary

leaders constructed the Declaration of Independence and the Constitution. Many of the words they used were explicitly biblical. For example, in the first paragraph of the Declaration, they premised their willingness to break from England on the right of people "to assume among the powers of the Earth, the separate and equal station to which the Laws of Nature and Nature's God entitle them." They "appeal[ed] to the Supreme Judge of the world for the rectitude of intentions," and then premised the rights the new government would give its citizens not on themselves, although they had drafted the Declaration, but on the "self-evident [truth] that all men are created equal, that they are *endowed by their Creator* [emphasis added] with certain unalienable rights."

The final words of the Declaration rise to a crescendo of faith and unity that all Americans would do well to read and embrace today:

> And for the support of this Declaration,
> with a firm reliance on the protection of
> divine Providence, we mutually pledge
> to each other our lives, our fortunes, and
> our sacred honor.

Over the almost 250 years of American history since 1776, the American government and succeeding generations of its leaders have recommitted our nation and people to that original vision of the God of the Bible, the source of America's national purpose and destiny.

Faith's Answers to America's Political Crisis

In the twentieth century, the United States emerged from World War II as the sole global superpower. It was the nation that had led the Allies to victory over fascism and Nazism and become the beacon of freedom and democracy throughout the world. Our faith-based vision of America soon became even more central to how we saw ourselves in the world and hoped others would see us, when the Soviet Communists became the greatest threat to the security and values of America and of our closest allies during the long Cold War.

In 1952, Dwight Eisenhower, a hero of World War II and then president-elect, declared: "Our form of government is based on the Judeo-Christian concept." During that same year, the Knights of Columbus, a Roman Catholic fraternal organization, began a campaign to add the words *under God* to the Pledge of Allegiance. Congressman Louis Rabaut, a Democrat from Michigan, was so moved by the Knights' campaign that he introduced legislation to add those words to the pledge. As detailed in congressional records from April 1953, he said those two words would give students and their parents "a deeper understanding of the real meaning of patriotism" and also would provide a "bulwark against communism."

President Eisenhower endorsed Rabaut's legislation. It passed, and he signed it into law on Flag Day, June 14, 1954. Two years later, Eisenhower made "In God We Trust" America's official national motto. Some will say that those

13

two laws were just about six more words, *under God* and *in God we trust*, but they resoundingly returned America to the faith-based vision that had guided and emboldened our Founding Fathers in 1776.

In our time, the foundational role of God in our government and politics seems too often to be forgotten or ignored by the American people and our elected leaders. The irony is that most of them are people of faith in their personal lives, but when they engage in politics and government, they seem to leave their faith in God and its values behind. They treat their fellow Americans who happen to be in another political party with gross disrespect; too often they demean each other personally; they spread lies or half-truths about each other; they are persistently uncivil toward each other, and frequently vicious. They don't have the mutual respect and courage to compromise with each other in order to get things done for our country and their constituents. Politicians fear losing the next election more than they fear finishing their careers without having done anything to make America a more perfect union. They are risk-averse. They would rather play it safe and get reelected than take a political risk to get something big and good done.

As a result, public opinion surveys make clear that the American people have never been more pessimistic about our country's future, angrier about our government, and less trusting of our leaders. Public opinion of the two major political parties that dominate our government and of the people who lead its executive, legislative, and judicial branches are at all-time lows. We are divided as a people more than at any time since the Civil War.

Today, America's government only rarely works to solve our biggest problems at home and abroad. Our credibility in the world has diminished seriously, and that jeopardizes our security and freedom. In the chapters that follow, I will appeal to the citizens of America, the people they elect to lead and represent them, and the media who report on their activities to think with me about the ways our shared faith in God can lead us to change our political behavior. I pray that I will be able to effectively convey this message to each reader, and that God will bless America and help us all find our way back to a better future together for our great country.

CHAPTER TWO

Partisanship

In this and the following chapters, I will focus on one element of America's current political crisis and then ask what our faith can teach us about how to reduce or eliminate that problem.

I begin with partisanship—primarily the dominant and divisive influence of the Democratic and Republican Parties—because their most active members are more loyal to their party and ideology than to our country. That in turn makes it very hard for elected officials to work with members of the other party to get things done.

In his Farewell Address in 1796, President George Washington explicitly warned Americans not to let political parties ever become too powerful and divisive—the very things they have in fact become:

> The unity of Government, which constitutes you one people—is a main pillar

in the edifice of your real independence, the support of your tranquility at home, your peace abroad, of your safety, of your prosperity, of that very liberty that you so highly prize.... All [separate] combinations and associations...serve to organize faction and to give it artful and extraordinary force; to put in the place of the delegated will of the nation, the will of a party, often a small but artful and enterprising minority of the community: and, accordingly to the alternate triumphs of different parties, to make the public administration the mirror of ill-concerted and incongruous projects of faction, rather than the organ of consistent and wholesome plans digested by common counsels, and modified by mutual interests.

The common and continual mischiefs of the spirit of party are sufficient to make it the interest and duty of a wise people to discourage and restrain it.

President Washington spoke those words almost 250 years ago, but, except for the old English style and vocabulary, they are a perfect warning to our elected leaders today.

Faith's Answers to America's Political Crisis

It is impressive that Washington so clearly saw how partisanship could divide and weaken America, because during his presidency the parties were in their infancy. That is why he referred to them as "factions." As time went on, the factions became parties, and eventually they were narrowed down to two parties—the Federalists and the Whigs. After Lincoln's election in 1860, the Whigs ceased to exist and were replaced by the new Republican Party. The Federalists had by then become known as Democrats. And that's the way it has stayed since—Republicans and Democrats. Neither the Constitution nor any statute requires the creation of political parties in America, and certainly not just the two we have now. They just grew organically, and for a long time that worked for our country, because both parties understood that at some point they had a responsibility to stop competing with each other and start working together to find common-ground solutions to big national problems and to create programs to seize big new national opportunities.

When I studied political science in college, I was taught that the two major American parties played a constructive role in our political system by bringing factions together in this very diverse country to form a working majority that could govern. On balance, the historic evidence justifies that positive evaluation of the Republicans and Democrats. But unfortunately, in our time, all that has changed. The two parties, as Harvard professor Michael Porter has said, have become a "duopoly" that dominates American politics and limits any competition to themselves for themselves. Although the political parties are not established by our Constitution or laws, they have nonetheless enacted laws and rules, particularly at the state level, that preserve their duopoly. For example, there are laws and party rules that govern the nomination of candidates by the two parties and determine who can participate in those nominations; other laws make it difficult for third parties to qualify for state ballots, including in presidential elections. And both parties have adopted rules that establish their control of legislative bodies, including Congress and most state legislatures.

In the US Senate, for example, even if you are elected as an Independent, which I was in 2006, the pressures are great to join one of the two political party caucuses because, according to Senate rules, the party caucuses enforce the seniority system, decide committee assignments and committee leadership, and work within their own party membership to shape and implement the legislative priorities of Congress. If you are not a member of the Democratic or Republican caucus, it is therefore unlikely you will be a truly productive senator for your constituents.

The accumulation of such power by the parties would be tolerable if they were still functioning as broad-based coalitions of smaller factions, and if they were still willing to work with members of the other party to find bipartisan solutions to national problems. But they are not. The right in the Republican Party and the left in the Democratic Party dominate their parties and rarely find their way to the center together.

Much has been written and spoken about why this has happened, and so I will not do more here than list the reasons given, all of which make sense to me. First is the gerrymandering of most House of Representatives districts to favor one party, so that in as many as 90 percent of the districts, the selection of their members of Congress is made on primary day, not on Election Day. This results in disproportionate influence by voters from the left in Democratic primaries and the right in Republican primaries, and prompts the natural political reflex of incumbents and challengers to defer to those "core constituencies" in their party to ensure that they win the primary.

Second is the growing partisanship of the media, which encourages officeholders to give cable channels and social media sites and their audiences the partisan or ideological messages they want to hear, so they can be asked to be on those channels and sites again. And third is the role of the parties and interest groups as major sources of ever-larger campaign contributions, which inevitably makes elected officials more dependent on their party and less willing to disagree with it.

The result is that nominations to federal office are controlled by a minority of members of each of the two major parties, and the rest of the candidates are left out and naturally become angry or apathetic. The trust of the citizenry, which is critical to the health of democracy, has been greatly diminished, and the bonds that have tied the American people together for so long have been seriously weakened.

We are living through George Washington's worst nightmares about American politics and government: members of political parties who put their loyalty to their party or "faction" first. The domestic political result among the American people has been unprecedented popular disaffection from the two major political parties, a profound distrust in government, and deepening public pessimism. In recent years, a consistent two-thirds or more of Americans tell pollsters they believe our country is going in the wrong direction.[1] That is very different from the optimism that has been characteristic of America during most of our history, and it shapes the current foul public mood.

Around the world, friends and foes see our disunity and are influenced by it. Their reaction depends on whether they are allies or enemies.

In his Farewell Address, President Washington warned that growing partisanship would compromise America's independence, which was still uncertain when he spoke at the end of the eighteenth century. Today, our independence is secure, but the extreme partisanship and disunity of our time have already crippled our domestic politics, threatened

---

1   The October 2023 Associated Press–NORC Center Poll found 78 percent thought our country is headed in the wrong direction.

our democracy, and compromised our international security and prosperity.

What then does our shared faith teach us about how we can control today's runaway partisanship? It begins, as always, with our faith in God, and with Abraham, who made the covenant with God that Jews, Christians, and Muslims believe in. Those bonds of shared paternity in God and Abraham should, of course, be much more important to each of us than today's divisive appeals for mindless political party loyalty.

The disunity caused by the fierce loyalty to party and ideology of right and left weakens our country at home and throughout the world. I believe it is also sacrilegious and contrary to our most important religious beliefs. The Bible is full of condemnations of sacrilegious acts that would cover today's misplaced loyalty to party over country. The word *sacrilege* itself comes from two Latin words: *sacer*, meaning "sacred," and *legere*, meaning "to steal." In its early usage, the word *sacrilege* applied to thieves who stole articles of value from tombs, but it came to mean any stealing or undercutting of sacredness in a place of worship, or the theft of a religious object.

The Hebrew Bible requires punishment for anyone who compromises the sanctity of the Temple of Jerusalem (Leviticus 17:1–9). The most memorable example of that rule is the death of the two sons of Aaron, the high priest, because they offered a "strange fire" in the temple. In modern Israel, there is a law requiring up to seven years of imprisonment for anyone convicted of profaning a holy place (of Judaism and other faiths) or violating its sanctity in any manner.

Jesus taught that the temple and everything connected with it were ordained by God, so any oath made in the temple was effectively made to God.

People in politics and government who are faithful believers in God need to ask themselves whether by making their political opponents, their fellow children of God, into enemies they are dishonoring God.

It might be asked whether political parties and ideologies have themselves become like gods to many political activists and leaders—like idols that are worshipped in violation of the Second Commandment that states we shall have no other gods but God.

When I was in college at Yale, I heard the chaplain, Reverend William Sloane Coffin, give a characteristically bold and progressive sermon based on the Second Commandment and on the following words from Deuteronomy 11:

> Take care lest your heart be deceived, and
> you turn aside and serve other gods and
> worship them; then the anger of the Lord
> will be kindled against you. (ESV)

Coffin argued that the words *other gods* did not mean just deities other than God, or physical idols. These words should also be understood, he preached, as a warning not to make gods out of sacrilegious behaviors, including materialism, power, racism, immorality, and violence. Today, we can add extreme loyalty to one's political party to that list of idols that must not be worshipped.

Some will question whether it goes too far from the biblical text to think of political partisanship and ideological extremism as acts of idolatry. But if we think about the way these acts divide God's children in America and make it so difficult for our government to function, to uphold the rule of law, to protect the national interest, and to help the least among us who need government's help, is it really wrong to argue that such partisanship and extremism are sacrilegious acts of idol worship?

The way to get our political conduct back in line with our religious beliefs is by putting God and country ahead of party and ideology. Once we do that, the next step is to unify the American people again. I believe that unity still underlies America, but that it has been suppressed by all the divisive factors I have cited. We must act to liberate our unity from the political conflict and partisan attack-and-counterattack media that dominate our public life today. Beneath all that noise and bitterness is a unity that you can see when Americans stand together at a public event, like a sports event, and sing "The Star-Spangled Banner" or "God Bless America," or say the Pledge of Allegiance. And you can also see it in the countless community, civic, charitable, and religious organizations in which Americans are working together with and for their neighbors every day. But you don't see it often anymore in American politics.

In politics and government, we have to learn again how to disagree without demeaning each other, and to remember that people in the other party or on the other side of any issue are not people to be hated or feared. They are our fellow Americans and fellow children of God who are as loved by God as we are, and those connections we have with each other are much more important than any political or ideological disagreements.

It is very important for us to get our national and personal priorities right again. As scriptures make clear, when kings ruled Israel, they were told that there were powers greater than themselves, namely God and the Bible.

The Revelation at Sinai provides a model for reaching that high level of understanding. The family of Jacob who had gone to Egypt four centuries before—fewer than one hundred people—went to Sinai as a mixed multitude of more than two million people. But they had not yet really become a nation. They were just a big tribe. Nationhood would come after they received the Ten Commandments, and with it their national values and purpose. At that historic moment, as the Israelites assembled at the foot of Mount Sinai to receive God's word, they achieved a necessary prerequisite for nationhood. They were unified, and they declared in one voice: "All that the Lord has spoken, we will do." (Exodus 19:8 ESV) The great medieval Jewish commentator Rashi described the two million Israelites at Sinai at that moment as "one person with one heart."

Over the centuries, commentators have added another important dimension to this moment. Although the Israelites were unified at Sinai, the Revelation was naturally understood and appreciated by every individual there in a personal and unique way. So, there was unity but not uniformity of opinion at Sinai.

That too is what we need to understand and aspire to in our country now. We need to restore national unity without expecting or, at worst, mandating, uniformity of ideas or policies. That has been the American way at our best in the past, and it can be again in our future if we put God and country first.

CHAPTER THREE

Political and Governmental Reform Will Not Happen Without Strong Leaders

Although the people have the ultimate power in our democratic republic to change our government, we also urgently need leaders who are willing to take on the failed status quo and accept the political and personal risks that will entail. We need leaders who are ready to serve a cause larger than themselves and their reelection.

There have not been many elected officials in recent times who have shown that kind of principled political courage. But there have been some, and it is important to give them the credit they deserve and give the rest of us hope that we will see more of such leadership. Two recent examples are Liz Cheney, a Republican, and Henry Cuellar, a Democrat.

Liz Cheney was elected to represent Wyoming in the US House of Representatives in 2016 and rose to become chair of the House Republican Conference, the third-highest position in the House Republican leadership. She was and is a leading ideological conservative. But she became increasingly offended by the behavior of former president Donald Trump after his defeat in the 2020 election. Although she knew Trump had carried Wyoming in that election with almost 70 percent of the vote, and therefore if she spoke out against him, it would put her political future in Wyoming in peril, she decided the rule of law and the health of democracy in America were worth the political risk.

She began to speak out against Trump's claim that the 2020 election had been stolen from him, and against his role in the violent attacks on the US Capitol on January 6, 2021, to stop the counting of the electoral votes. In the end, she voted with the Democrats to impeach Trump for his behavior on January 6.

All that courageous behavior infuriated most of her House Republican colleagues, and so they removed her from the House Republican leadership. After she agreed to serve as vice chair of the House Select Committee on the January 6 attack, she was censured by the Republican National Committee, and on August 16, 2022, in the Republican primary for her congressional seat, Cheney lost the nomination to a candidate Trump had endorsed.

If somebody were to write an updated version of President Kennedy's *Profiles in Courage*, Liz Cheney would deserve a chapter. In fact, on May 22, 2022, she received the

JFK Profile in Courage Award from the John F. Kennedy Library Foundation.

Less visible but equally deserving is Henry Cuellar, a Democrat who has represented Texas' twenty-eighth district in Congress since 2005. His voting record has been center-right, unusual for a Democrat. His consistently strong pro-life statements and votes have made him different in the Democratic caucus, and ultimately were the reason he faced a very strong primary challenge in 2022 from Jessica Cisneros, who was supported by progressive, pro-choice political groups with campaign contributions and workers. Cuellar, on the other hand, was essentially abandoned by the leadership of his Democratic Party, but he nevertheless resisted all pressure to change or modify the beliefs he held, which were rare among his fellow Democrats. In other words, Henry Cuellar put his political future on the line by refusing to change what he thought was right. In the June 2021 primary, Cuellar won the nomination by 289 votes, proving it is still possible to be "different" in politics and be reelected.

The need for leaders to bring about change is a powerful lesson from our three Abrahamic religions and their leaders. Abraham, Jesus, and Muhammad had the faith and courage to go against what existed before them. They were leaders who took risks and fought the status quo to uphold and advance their faith in God and the values they believed came with it. They had the courage to be different, and that is why they changed the world.

> For if the trumpet give an uncertain
> sound, who shall prepare himself to the
> battle? (1 Corinthians 14:8 KJV)

The three great monotheistic faiths began with God's invocation to Abraham, the father of nations, in Genesis 12:1:

> Go from your country and your kindred
> and your father's house to the land that I
> will show you. (ESV)

Remember that the Bible tells us that God chose Abraham because He found his heart to be faithful and loyal to Him. God gave him a clear directive:

> ...[to] command his children and his
> household after him to keep the way of
> the Lord by doing righteousness and jus-
> tice. (Genesis 18:19 ESV)

Jesus and Muhammad each received calls from God and took action against the religious and political status quo of their place and time. Jesus challenged the civil and religious power structure in Jerusalem. Muhammad convinced the idol worshippers of Arabia to believe in one God, then won a military victory over his opponents in Mecca, and ultimately united the people of Arabia in devotion to Allah. Abraham, Jesus, and Muhammad were great teachers as well as great leaders, and that is why their faith in one God is shared today by the majority of people on Earth.

The other great lesson the Bible teaches leaders is that with the power they have accumulated comes not the freedom to do whatever they want, but a greater responsibility to do what they should. They must be the best role models they can be, because the authority and visibility that come with being a leader mean that their behavior will have a great influence on the behavior of their followers. The Bible provides several moving examples of this strict rule of behavior for leaders.

When the prophet Samuel takes the crown from King Saul because he has failed to follow the instructions of God in dealing with the Amalekites, Samuel teaches Saul and every political leader since:

> Though you are little in your own eyes...
> the Lord anointed you king over Israel.
> (1 Samuel 15:17 ESV)

Saul's response is to make excuses. He argues that he failed to follow God's directions because the people wanted to do otherwise. That, of course, is not an acceptable excuse for a leader. It is, in fact, an admission by Saul that he is not a good leader. Saul's failure was that he yielded to the political demands of the masses around him, instead of having the courage to tell them they must do what was right—what God wanted them to do.

That same failure to follow God's commandments instead of yielding to the politically popular and easy course almost ended the history of the Israelites on Mount Sinai (rather than it all just beginning there). Moses had gone up the mountain to receive the Ten Commandments. When he had not returned forty days later, the Israelites feared that he would never come back, and panicked. To pacify them, Aaron committed a grave sin. He allowed them to make and worship an idol, a calf of gold. When God saw this, He was furious and declared that He would destroy all the people, including Aaron, who had enabled them to sin. Only after Moses pleaded with God to give the Israelites, including his brother, a second chance, did He relent, and the history of the Israelites, including the Ten Commandments, was allowed to continue.

Moses is the most poignant example of a great leader who was punished by God for one moment of failure. He was prohibited by God from entering the Holy Land, because in his anger at the Israelites for complaining about a lack of water, he struck the rock instead of speaking to it, as God had explicitly directed him. For this, he was prohibited from entering Israel and could see the Holy Land only from afar.

From its earliest chapters, the Bible also makes clear that people—not just leaders—must take responsibility for their actions and not make excuses for behavior that they know is wrong. When God confronts Adam and Eve because they have done the one thing He told them not to do—eat the forbidden fruit from the Tree of Knowledge of Good and Evil—Adam blames Eve, and Eve blames the serpent (Genesis 3:9–12).

After Cain kills Abel, God asks him, "Where is your brother?" And Cain lies, "I don't know. Am I my brother's keeper?"

We can almost hear God shouting back at Cain when we read His words in the Bible: "What have you done? The voice of your brother's blood is crying to me from the ground" (Genesis 4:8–10 ESV). As a result of eating the forbidden fruit, Adam and Eve are banished from the paradise of Eden, Cain is condemned to wander the earth, and humanity's future is radically limited because of their failure to take responsibility for their actions.

These are important lessons from the Bible for our leaders today if our leaders are to take us out of our current political morass. We need leaders who will not yield to what seems popular in order to protect themselves. We need leaders who will be brave enough to be different.

In 1787, Thomas Jefferson wrote to James Madison:

> I hold it that a little rebellion now and then is a good thing, and as necessary in the political world as storms in the physical.

We are now at a time in American history when we need at least "a little rebellion." Our two-party political system is not working to benefit the citizenry because the parties have grown much more powerful and much less responsible over time. Each is controlled by a core group of members who are ideologically unrepresentative of the majority of the American people, and of a lot of people in their own party.

It is not surprising that the American people have turned against the two parties and that, according to a September 2023 Gallup poll, the largest and fastest-growing political party in America is no party—Independents. Two of the worst consequences of the deepening antagonism between America's two major political parties are that they spend so much time throwing partisan and ideological rocks at each other that we have lost confidence in them, and that they have lost the ability and will to trust each other. Without trust, the parties who control Congress and the White House are unable to come together, even at times of greatest national crisis, as they have in the past, when they would talk and listen to each other respectfully and then find common-sense, common-ground compromises that could be enacted into law.

There are other bad consequences of the warfare between Republicans and Democrats in Washington besides political ones; there are cultural, psychological, and sociological ones. For example, the prominence of political leaders who are in constant combat with each other not only divides our people; it also depresses us and produces a disengaged citizenry. Because many of America's elected leaders attack each other in the most personally disrespectful and vulgar language, their words also have the effect of making our society in general more uncivilized and lowering the language of people toward each other. That affects everyone, including our children. Sometimes it seems as if the behavior of our political leaders has given us permission to leave the world of civil and respectful relations, and instead verbally abuse each other and sometimes physically abuse each other, as on January 6, 2021, at the US Capitol. Instead of expressing respectful differences of opinion, too many Americans go right for the jugular and spew hatred that leaves wounds and scars and division.

Today we urgently need leaders—Independents, Republicans, and Democrats—who will be motivated and guided by the leadership of role models Abraham, Jesus, and Muhammad. We need leaders who will be able to find the strength that enabled those three great leaders to be different, and to find the courage and capability to move people to change. The following are personal qualities and goals that I believe political leaders who want to take us out of our current crisis should embrace in their public service, so they will become better role models.

Self-confidence. The rabbis of old taught that we should imagine that God has given us two pieces of paper, one for each hand. On one it is written, "The world was created for you, and so you are capable of achieving great things." The other says, "You are no bigger than a small speck of sand on a beach." In other words, each of us should have a combination of confidence in how we can improve the world and humility about how much we can accomplish alone. Leaders should aspire to have the courage of King David, the humility of Moses, and the vision of both.

Purpose. Our most important religious texts and the best leaders who speak to us from them teach us to have a vision that looks beyond the status quo to something better. In the case of American politics and government, the most important goal for our leaders is clear: they must give us policies we can believe in and work together again to make our government work for us. We need to put our national values and national purpose ahead of any party's policies and any personal ideology. That does not mean abandoning our beliefs or dropping our membership in a political party. It means sustaining those beliefs and that membership, but putting our larger American values and interests first.

Trust. When I entered Connecticut politics, an older political leader gave me advice that seemed simplistic at the time, but became sensible and wise to me over the years. He said, "In politics, your word is your bond. To get anything done, you need to make agreements with other politicians that you and they can rely on. There are no written contracts to enforce those agreements or laws to punish someone who breaks an agreement. But if you come to be known as a politician who doesn't keep his word, others will not trust you, and your ability to get anything done will drop to zero.

Your constituents and fellow politicians and public servants have to trust you, and, of course, you have to trust them."

Henry L. Stimson, America's secretary of war during the Second World War and after, built on that idea when he said, "The chief lesson I have learned in a long life is that the only way you can make a man trustworthy is to trust him: and the surest way to make him untrustworthy is to distrust him."

One of the greatest casualties of our current partisan and ideological conflict is trust among our leaders. They do not spend enough nonpolitical time together to get to know each other and trust each other. The times they do spend in the same place are heavy with partisan politics and attacks and counterattacks. In my years in the Senate, my closest and most productive relationships were with colleagues I spent non-Senate time with, so that we learned about each other outside the standard political discourse. We developed trust in each other.

Stimson's advice to our leaders and all of us is very wise. We can restore the trust that is necessary to protect and strengthen our democracy by an initial act of trusting some-one we do not now trust.

Civility. Increasing incivility, including the use of abu-sive language without limits, is one of the greatest causes of the prevailing distrust and resulting division and gridlock in our government. Politicians didn't create the incivility and foul language that are so common in our society, but they have made the problem worse by bringing these things into the public square.

All religions teach us about the power of words to raise us up or knock us down, and all religions chasten their followers who speak or write about one another without discipline. Those are lessons our leaders must think about and follow. There is a wonderful story in the Talmud of a man who went to a rabbi and admitted that he had been speaking dishonestly and disrespectfully about the rabbi. The man wanted to make amends. What should he do? The rabbi told him to go home, take a down-filled pillow outside, cut the pillowcase, and let the feathers fly out. The man was puzzled but did as the rabbi instructed, and then reported back to say he hoped that it would be considered an act of penitence and an apology. The rabbi then told him to go out and find the feathers and put them back into the pillow. The man naturally protested that it would be an impossible task. And the rabbi said, "I know it is impossible, just as it is impossible for you to recapture the false and vicious words you have spoken, which have by now spread as far and wide as the feathers in your pillow. The best you can do is never again speak badly and falsely about any other person."

Since the birth of America in the eighteenth century, there have been spirited exchanges between our political leaders. But never have there been such lies, slander, and personal attacks in public life as now. And, of course, we have never before had the capacity the digital age provides to share our lies and slander with the world. It will not be easy or quick to end the incivility and destructive language in American politics and public life. In fact, it might be even harder than finding the feathers from that pillow. In a society that fortunately gives constitutional protection to freedom of speech, the best way to control our language about each other is to do it ourselves. We should do it because all of our religions tell us it is the right thing to do, but also, of course, because it will improve our country, government, and lives in many ways.

Because of extreme partisanship and loss of civility and trust, American politicians are no longer having the kind of debates that are at the heart of a democracy, in which people disagree without demeaning each other, listen to each other and, when justified, acknowledge that the other side actually has made a good point. Then they can even sit and reason together in the spirit of Isaiah (11:18 ESV):

> "Come now, let us reason together," says the Lord, "though your sins are like scarlet, they shall be as white as snow; though they are red like crimson, they shall become like wool."

In Judaism, a process very much like that is the way the Talmud, the code of laws that governs the religious and ethical life of Jews, came into being. It was developed over centuries of discussion and debate among rabbis in response to questions they posed to each other and questions people asked them about how to apply sections of the Bible to their lives.

American political and government leaders, and our democracy, desperately need more of that kind of debate today—debate that ends not in more division and hatred, but in more mutual respect, consensus, and progress.

CHAPTER FOUR

Incivility

*C**ivility**,* according to the dictionary, means "politeness and courtesy in speech or behavior." But civility needs to mean much more than that in our politics today, as is suggested by its Latin roots. The Latin origin of the word *civility* is *civilis*, which comes from *civis*, meaning "citizen." *Civilis* also has sometimes been defined as "courtesy befitting a fellow citizen." These Latin roots suggest that civility is not meant to apply just to personal manners in private, but should define our relations with other citizens in our society. Civility, in other words, is an important building block of a collaborative and unified country. In the same way, incivility is not just an act of personal discourtesy, insult, or vulgarity toward others. It is one of the significant causes of division in a country and dysfunction in governments, because uncivil behavior undercuts trust among people, which is a necessary precondition of a healthy democracy and unified country.

It is beyond debate that incivility has grown dramatically in America in recent decades. Why? Cultural norms change over time in a society, and that undoubtedly is part of the reason. But I believe that changes in our entertainment culture and the uncivil conduct of too many of our political leaders have made the problem much worse.

When I was growing up in the 1950s and 1960s, the content of movies and the language spoken on the screen were tightly controlled by the motion picture industry, according to its Hays Code—the purpose of which was to respect America's mainstream values and therefore not deter people from going to the movies. The Hays Code prohibited "profanity, suggestive nudity, graphic or realistic violence, sexual persuasions, and rape" in movies from 1930 to 1968. In 1975, the Federal Communications Commission (FCC) required broadcast television stations to provide a family hour every evening from 8 to 9 p.m., so parents could watch television with their children without fear that the kids would see violent or sexual programming or hear profane language.

Cable television was not controlled by the FCC and therefore when it came along did not have to follow the family-hour requirements or most other content limitations. Once cable television got bigger audiences for its entertainment that could not appear on the broadcast networks during the family hour, the broadcast networks reacted to the new competition by abandoning the family hour. The motion picture industry had already replaced the Hays Code with a ratings system, which ended the taboos of the code but warned people about what they were about to see and hear. These changes definitely helped make America more uncivil.

When the internet arrived and people could communicate without limits to each other and the world, the civility that characterized our society became a piece of history. The Hays Code and the family hour on television may seem outdated now, but I believe America was a healthier and surely more civil society when they were in effect.

America's politicians mimicked the increasing incivility in society by becoming more uncivil themselves. They no longer treated each other with the same respect; of course, the simultaneous increase in partisanship in our politics also helped end civility. Now the lowering of political speech and debate has further divided our country, and that is a big cause of our political crisis today.

But if you go back and read the language of our early political leaders, it is the Queen's English—sometimes personal, sometimes judgmental, but always formal, respectful, and civil. That's pretty much the balance that was maintained until recent decades, when the mix of declining societal and entertainment culture civility, the mass digitalization of communications, and the changing behavior of politicians who didn't lead but followed those developments lowered our political discourse and divided our country. In the US Senate, for example, traditional formalities, such as referring to a fellow senator as "my distinguished colleague from…" have continued, but too often they are followed by words directed at that senator that are personal and harsh. Campaigns for elective office are dominated by negative advertising on social media and television that attacks the other candidate in the most brutal ways, sometimes based on facts, sometimes distorting facts, and sometimes without any basis in fact. Citizens are not urged to vote for the candidate sponsoring the ad as much as to vote against his or her opponent.

As a result, our democracy suffers. People develop negative feelings toward both major parties, the candidates they are running, and the political system that has produced them. If Walmart and Target spent all their advertising budgets attacking each other, fewer people would shop at either chain. Yet that is what is happening with Democrats and Republicans today. The all-time high of disaffiliation from the two major parties is a market reaction to their failures. It should wake them up and lead them to change, but obviously it has not yet.

Maybe a reawakening of religious faith among our politicians and people can begin to roll back the corrosive incivility of our culture, country, and politics.

The first step that elected officials, and the people who control the news media and spread and exploit the incivility that exists in politics, should take might seem irrelevant: go back to God. If you believe in God, the Creator, then you believe that every one of us—and that means every politician in any party, with any ideology—is a member of the same human family and is "entitled" not just to "life, liberty, and the pursuit of happiness" but to respect and civility. That is a transcendent and profound truth that most Americans hold in their hearts and heads and bring to their houses of worship, but it seems to be forgotten in the everyday swirl of careers, businesses, campaigns, and the quest for power or profits.

Stepping back and understanding that our belief in God and the values that flow from it are more important than the pressures and temptations we face to be uncivil to one another would be the best way to begin to rebuild America's civility. It doesn't mean we should avoid disagreements. It means we should be civil to one another when we disagree.

One of the most important religious values that should guide politicians to treat each other more civilly is the Golden Rule:

> "Love your neighbor as yourself" (Leviticus 19:18 ESV).

> "Thou shalt love thy neighbor as thyself" (Matthew 22:39 KJV).

> "None of you has faith until he loves for his brother or his neighbor what he loves for himself" (Sahih Muslim 1:72).

Senator Joe Lieberman

"Do naught unto others which would cause you pain if done to you" (Golden Rule of *dharma* in Hinduism).

The Golden Rule calls out to politicians to stop attacking other politicians in ways they do not want to be attacked themselves.

Every God-centered religion urges its members to emulate God's characteristics as best we humans can. God sets high moral and legal standards for better behavior, but is also merciful and forgiving when people do not meet those standards, as in the case of the golden calf on Mount Sinai. If God could forgive the Israelites for such a terrible sin, American politicians can break the cycle of incivility and hatred with other politicians by being merciful and forgiving and moving on to the next topic of discussion.

During the 1990s, I worked alongside congressional colleagues in both parties to pressure the people who own and operate our entertainment industries to adopt codes and improve rating systems to protect our children. We had some significant success with that focus on children. But it will take more than better ratings systems to bring America back to civility. It will take individual decisions by political leaders to act civilly. It also will take the realization by people with power in the entertainment and news businesses that there is a better way to do what they do than by producing and broadcasting the worst of human speech and behavior and thereby spreading it among millions of viewers and listeners. The words we use can elevate or lower us and our country. They can heal or hurt, unify or divide. They can express love or hate, hope or pessimism, truth or lies. We will not reduce the incivility of our society and our politics unless we apply discipline and values to the way we use the gift of speech God has given us.

Our religions and our religious texts could not be clearer about how consequential speech is, and therefore how important it is for us to use it wisely and respectfully. In the Bible, even the act of divine Creation is accomplished with speech: "And God *said* [emphasis added], 'Let there be light,' and there was light" (Genesis 1:3 ESV).

Those words, "And God *said* [emphasis added]…. And there was…," are repeated for each of the six days of Creation.

The Revelation and the giving of the Ten Commandments also occurred through words. As Moses reminds the Israelites, "The Lord *spoke* [emphasis added] to you out of the midst of the fire. *You heard the sound of words*, but saw no form; there was only a voice" (Deuteronomy 4:12 ESV).

Two of the Ten Commandments are mandates for good and appropriate speech in our relations with God and our fellow humans. In the Third Commandment, we are told, "Do not take the name of the Lord Your God in vain." And in the Ninth Commandment: "Do not testify as a false witness."

The one-sentence affirmation of faith that Jews are called to recite in prayer twice each day and say before death is: "*Hear*, [emphasis added] O Israel: The Lord our God, the Lord is one" (Deuteronomy 6:4 ESV).

As we have discussed, when Jesus is asked what the essence of his faith is, he answers with those same words: "The first of all the commandments *is*: '*Hear*, [emphasis added] O Israel, the Lord our God, the Lord is one'" (Mark 12:29–31 NKJV).

In each of the three daily prayer services of Judaism, there is a silent prayer in which congregants speak personally with God and hope He hears them. That prayer begins and ends with appeals about language. At the beginning, we say to God: "Open my lips and my mouth will praise you." At the end: "Guard my tongue from saying bad things and prevent my lips from speaking dishonestly." And then we add: "Let my soul be quiet and ignore those who curse me."

The Bible itself is also very clear, not just about the importance of words and listening and hearing them clearly, but about what we say with words:

> "Keep yourself far from a false matter" (Exodus 23:7 NKJV).

> "You shall not go about *as* a talebearer among your people" (Leviticus 19:16 NKJV).

Words like these might well be placed on the walls of both chambers of Congress, on the front door of every campaign headquarters, and on the screen saver of every computer in every political consulting firm and newsroom in America.

In Christianity, the importance of proper and civil speech is repeatedly stated. In Luke 6:45, Jesus says:

> The good person out of the good treasure of his heart produces good and the evil person out of his evil treasure produces evil, for out of the abundance of the heart, his mouth speaks.

Paul tells the Ephesians that words can destroy or build and exhorts them: "Let each one of you speak the truth with his neighbor." (Ephesians 4:25 ESV) And John declares that lying is a sin and the work of the enemy (John 8:44).

The Prophet Muhammad said: "Whoever believes in Allah and the last day should either speak what is good or remain silent." In the Quran (49:12), Allah says, "O you who have believed, avoid [negative] assumptions...and do not...backbite each other."

In Judaism, a whole ethic about language has been built up from the prescriptions in the Bible about speech, particularly the prohibition in Leviticus (19:16 NKJV) to "not go about *as* a talebearer among your people." Based on those words, the rabbis hold that a person should not say something negative about someone else even if it's true, unless there is an urgent reason for the person being targeted to know. Of course, if what you are saying about another person is not true, it is a grave sin; in Hebrew that sin is called *lashon hara*, meaning "evil tongue." Some rabbis even hold that untruthful gossip is like murder because its impact on the person who is slandered can be like death. "Cursed be anyone who strikes down his neighbor in secret," Moses says in Deuteronomy 27:24 (ESV), and the rabbis interpret those words as referring to slander.

These faith-based rules of speech are strong and clear. If politicians, most of whom believe in God and the Bible, would apply them to what they say about their opponents, it would go a long way to bringing civility back into politics, and with it a renewed trust in and unity within government.

This transformation will happen only if people in positions of power in politics, government, and the news media make the moral choice to make it happen. It will require self-discipline and self-regulation of speech for a larger purpose, which is to restore civility in our country so that our people can be reunited and our government can work again. We will not restore civility to our society by governmental mandates or the workings of the markets. It is up to individuals to choose civility over incivility. Moses says in his final message to the Israelites before his death, "This day I call the heavens and the earth as witnesses against you that I have set before you life and death, blessings and curses. Now choose life, so that you and your children may live" (Deuteronomy 30:19 NIV).

Today, we should also say to our political leaders: "Now choose civility, so that you and your children and ours may live better lives in a better country."

CHAPTER FIVE

Distrust

The negative forces in American politics and government that we have discussed—partisanship, incivility, and divisive media—have all contributed to an unprecedented loss of trust. And that matters a lot in a democracy such as ours.

In a dictatorship in which the leader and the government tell all citizens what they must do all the time, trust is unnecessary. Everything is up to the dictator. All that is required from the rest is subservience to the dictator's will. A democracy and the freedom it promises cannot work without trust between the elected leaders and their constituents, and among the elected leaders themselves. The leaders need to work together and reach agreements so that the government can do what the country and its people need it to do. The undercutting of trust in American politics that results from putting party loyalty ahead of the national interest is the greatest cause of the dysfunction of America's government.

Chief Rabbi Jonathan Sacks put this hurtful contemporary reality into the hopeful context of the Bible. His creative and instructive lesson is drawn from one of the closing chapters of the Book of Numbers (30:2 ASV):

> When a man voweth a vow unto the Lord, or sweareth an oath to bind his soul with a bond, he shall not break his word; he shall do according to all that proceedeth out of his mouth.

In his book *I Believe*, Rabbi Sacks asks why God directed Moses to convey these words about the importance of vows and oaths to the Israelites, as recounted at the end of the Book of Numbers, just before Moses begins his moving speech of farewell and guidance to them (in Deuteronomy). In other words, Rabbi Sacks is asking why the Bible puts this focus on mundane vows and oaths right before Moses' soaring poetic farewell. He answers his question with poetry of his own, which speaks directly to America's leaders today:

> Freedom needs trust; trust needs people to keep their word; and keeping your word means treating words as holy, and vows and oaths as sacrosanct.... That is why as the Israelites approached the Holy Land where they were to create a free society, they had to be reminded of

> the sacred character of vows and oaths....
> The moral is still relevant today. A free
> society depends on trust. Trust depends
> on keeping your word.

That lesson is not only relevant; it is urgently necessary for the maintenance of our security, prosperity, and freedom that our leaders and we the people overcome all that divides us to rebuild trust among us.

As I look back on my ten years in the Connecticut State Senate and twenty-four years in the US Senate, I appreciate that trust between my colleagues and me was fundamental to almost everything we were able to accomplish. In Connecticut, I had a friend who used to say, "In politics, there are no permanent allies and no permanent enemies. There are only temporary partnerships to solve particular problems." There was truth in that observation, of course, but the best and most productive relationships I had with colleagues were based on trust and were permanent. In Washington, DC, that was true of my relationships with, among others, Senators John McCain, Susan Collins, Harry Reid, and Chris Dodd.

The first time I heard the word *trust* after I was elected to the Connecticut State Senate in 1988, as a Democrat, was in a conversation with the newly elected Senate majority leader, George Mitchell of Maine. The first vote I cast as a senator was for Mitchell to be majority leader, and I always felt good about that. Mitchell was a man of the law who had served as a federal court judge before coming to the Senate. He became an important mentor to me.

In a meeting with him before I was formally sworn in as a senator in January 1989, Mitchell taught me something important that involved trust. He reminded me that there were one hundred members of the Senate, and that we were lucky that the American people had just elected fifty-five Democratic senators. But there would be hundreds of issues we would be dealing with in the Senate during the next two years, he continued, and every senator could not become an expert on every issue. So, we needed to rely on each other.

"Even though you are only a freshman in a chamber where seniority matters," he said, "if you chose two or three issues that are priorities for you, learn them well, and speak intelligently about them in the Democratic caucus and on the Senate floor, your fellow senators will come to trust you and vote the way you recommend or work with you on similar legislation in the future. That's the way you will be able to get a lot done here, even in your first year or two as a senator."

The four areas I chose were environmental protection, foreign policy, national security, and economic growth. Mitchell was right. I found that if I did my homework in those areas and presented my arguments well, my colleagues would trust me, and I was able to form alliances with senators of both parties, which helped me get a lot done.

Faith's Answers to America's Political Crisis

As I look back, I realize that I also encouraged a different kind of trust among my Republican Party colleagues during my early years in the Senate, because I was willing to break with the Democratic Caucus and vote with the Republicans if that was what I believed was right. For example, in 1990 after Saddam Hussein invaded Kuwait, I was the first Democratic senator to say I would support a resolution to authorize President Bush to use America's military to push Iraq out of Kuwait. That led the administration to ask me, even though I was only a freshman, to cosponsor that resolution with my Republican senior colleague John Warner of Virginia. It passed by five votes (fifty-two to forty-seven) but only, I am proud to say, because ten Democratic senators supported it. That experience created trust between my Republican colleagues and me, because they saw I was willing to break from my party based on a difference of opinion and was very unlikely to be pressured to change my mind once I did. That was a different kind of trust, but it also increased my effectiveness.

The debate on the Iraq War of 1991 was the first time John McCain and I worked together, and it began a wonderful personal friendship and Senate partnership based on trust that was built up with every cause we took on together, such as working to stop the aggression and genocide in the Balkans in the early 1990s, and every time we traveled together to visit our troops overseas or to meet with foreign leaders. We had a lot of time on planes to get to know each other personally, and to develop trust in each other, which is difficult in today's whirlwind, politically divided Senate. John and I hardly ever disagreed on any national security or foreign policy issues, but we had great differences of opinion on many domestic issues. These differences didn't matter, however, because we trusted each other.

In 2008, when John had locked up the Republican nomination for president, he put me on the short list to be vetted to run as his vice president. I told him that I didn't see how he could ever choose me, because—although I had been reelected to the Senate in 2006 as an Independent—I was still a registered Democrat. His response was, "That's the point. The country is sick of partisanship, and I think voters will really go for a bipartisan ticket." One of his most important advisers told me the same thing and added, "And John trusts you more than anyone else who could be his running mate this year."

Senator Susan Collins, Republican of Maine, and I began to work together because we both happened to serve on the Senate Governmental Affairs Committee, the Senate's major oversight and investigative committee. We soon saw that we were kindred spirits: both independents in our respective parties, both wanting to make our public service matter by getting legislation passed, and both understanding that getting legislation passed would be most likely to happen if we worked across party lines. When people asked me back then why Susan and I worked so well together, I would say simply: "We trust each other." That meant that we could rely on each other's word. If we disagreed on a policy and it looked like we could not compromise, we would be honest with the other about that and move on. Neither of us ever tried to jump out publicly in front of the other on an issue to get more publicity. We waited and did it together. We each knew the other was working hard to be informed on the issues, as George Mitchell had advised me to do, and we developed confidence in each other.

From 2003 to 2013, depending on which party was in the majority in the US Senate, I was either chair or ranking minority member of the Senate Governmental Affairs Committee, as was Susan Collins. I remember that at our first public hearing one year after the Democrats had retaken the majority and I became the committee chair, I said that the only thing that had changed was that Susan had turned the gavel over to me—and that otherwise, we would still operate as the equal, trusting legislative partners we had become.

My relationship with Susan enabled us to do some transformational work in response to the 9/11 terrorist attacks. Our committee recommended and saw through to enactment the creation of a bipartisan commission on 9/11 over opposition from the Bush administration and many Democratic committee chairs, all of whom wanted to do the investigation themselves.

When the commission issued its historic report, normal Senate procedure would have split it into pieces that would have gone to several subject matter committees. But the two top Senate leaders, Republican Bill Frist and Democrat Tom Daschle, decided that such a move would delay any Senate actions on the commission's recommendations, and probably even block some of the most important recommendations. So they gave our committee exclusive jurisdiction over the report because, as they said at the time, they *trusted* Susan and me to work together to get the commission's recommendations adopted as soon as possible.

That's exactly what Susan and I did, through tough negotiations in the Senate and the conference committee with the House, as well as with the Bush administration. And there is no question that one of the key factors in getting the recommendations adopted was that Susan and I were an unbreakable team throughout it all. We trusted each other. The result was the most significant reform in America's national security and intelligence agencies since the beginning of the Cold War in the late 1940s.

Chris Dodd and I got to know each other while working our way up in Connecticut politics. When I was elected to the Senate in 1988, Chris had already served there for eight years. On my first visit to Washington, after the election in late 1988, Chris gave me great advice about the transition to the Senate: "The worst relations between senators from the same state are surprisingly when they are members of the same party. They compete with each other for credit back home and for advancement here in the Senate. The result is that each is a less effective senator than he or she could be. You and I are not going to let that happen to us." And we didn't. As a result, we were able to get more done for Connecticut and its people, and we shared the public credit for that. We also helped each other rise in the inner world of the Senate. Chris and I trusted each other, and our colleagues and constituents knew that.

An unexpected example of the strength of our relationship happened in 2000 when I was vetted by Vice President Al Gore to be his running mate in the presidential election. The Gore campaign managers told me to tell no one that I was being vetted. But I had a problem. A few of the liberal interest groups in the Democratic Party were expressing concerns about my potentially being selected because although they considered me friendly, I was not automatically 100 percent committed to their interests. We decided I needed to ask someone to talk to those groups, and that the best person would be Chris Dodd. After a joint press conference in Branford, Connecticut, on a sunny summer day in 2000, I asked for help. He immediately agreed and added the wise words of a friend: "Joe, you never know if anything like this will happen again, and it would be irresponsible for you not to do everything you can within the rules the Gore campaign has set down to make it happen. I am glad to try to be of help."

A humorous coda to this story happened when I sat down for my final interview with Vice President Gore at his official residence in July 2000. He asked how certain liberal interest groups would react if he selected me. After the third time, my answer was: "Chris Dodd has talked to them, and they'll be OK." Al said, "Joe, is Chris Dodd now your John the Baptist?" We both laughed a lot at that Judeo-Christian humor.

Harry Reid was one of the most skillful, unusual, engaging people I ever met in politics. We developed a strong, practical, and—yes—trusting relationship. I always felt that Harry was there to help me if he could, and he knew I would help him if I could. When he became the leader of Senate Democrats, we had an agreement that was unwritten but airtight: I would tell him early if I could not take the Democratic Party position on a legislative proposal, and he would respect that. But he knew that if he really needed my vote on a bill and I did not have a strong personal position on it, he could count on my support. It worked for both of us.

After the 2008 presidential campaign, in which I supported John McCain, a few of my Democratic colleagues started a movement to take away my seniority and my committee chairmanship. Harry asked me to come to his office two days after the election, and he told me that he would have to respond to those angry Democratic senators and ask me to give up my Homeland Security chairmanship, but that he would offer me the chairmanship of a minor committee. I immediately told him that I could not accept that humiliation, because as he knew better than anyone, I had been a good member of the caucus and he had been able to count on me when he needed me, so as a result he could trust me.

Harry was silent for about fifteen seconds and then said, "That's what I thought you would say. OK. Now let's talk about how we're going to get you the votes to keep your seniority and chairmanship." Later that day, President-Elect Barack Obama issued a gracious statement saying he did not favor punitive action and there should be room for all Senate Democrats in our caucus. The next week, there was a closed Senate Democratic organizing caucus, which included a debate on a motion to strip me of my seniority and therefore my chairmanship. Harry opposed it, and it was roundly defeated by a vote of forty-two to thirteen.

In the years that followed, President Obama and Harry asked for my help in supporting and, where possible, helping them get support from moderate Republicans for the administration's priorities. This included the passage of the bill for economic recovery following the Great Recession of 2008 and the repeal of the "Don't Ask, Don't Tell" policy, which unjustly regulated the military service of gay and lesbian Americans. I was glad to help and am proud that I was able to make a difference for the better in enacting those important laws.

I have taken the time to tell these stories of how building relations of trust with Republicans and Democrats was so important to my ability to be an effective senator in the hope that they may encourage current and future members of Congress to do the same. If those political stories are not enough, let me return to the focus of this book and describe the priority that our religious texts give to the trust between God and humans, which should set a standard for us.

In the Hebrew Bible, the two most intimate relationships that God has with people are with Abraham and Moses. God made His original covenant with Abram and changed his name to Abraham, which means "father of nations." And God chose Moses to liberate the children of Israel and to lead them to Mount Sinai, where Moses received the Ten Commandments on their behalf and on behalf of all the people of the world.

Why did God choose Abraham?

> You are the Lord, the God who chose Abram and brought him out of Ur of the Chaldeans and gave him the name Abraham. You found his heart faithful before you, and made with him the covenant...
> (Nehemiah 9:7–8 ESV)

In other words, God *trusted* Abraham because He had confidence in his values and behavior:

> For I have chosen him; he will command his children and his household

> after him to keep the way of the Lord by
> doing righteousness and justice. (Genesis
> 18:17–19 ESV)

The biblical text is less clear about why God trusted Moses so much that He chose him to lead the children of Israel out of slavery to Mount Sinai and then to the Promised Land. It is true that Moses was raised in the palace of the pharaoh by the pharaoh's daughter, and therefore must have been educated and trained for leadership. But God's choice was based on more than that. It was based on Moses' behavior, as it was with Abraham. Before the angels of God called to Moses from the burning bush, he had already proven himself to be a person of justice and compassion. He had acted twice to stop one man from beating another. And perhaps even more important is the following story told in Exodus 3:1–14, and its expansion in the Midrash—a collection of rabbinical beliefs that fill in spaces in the Bible narrative:

> Moses was tending the flock of Jethro
> his father-in-law.… And he led the flock
> to the back of the desert, and came to
> Horeb [Sinai], the mountain of God.
> (NKJV)

It was there that Moses saw the burning bush and received the mission from God that would later bring him back to that mountain to receive the Ten Commandments. In the commentary on this section in the Midrash, Moses is drawn to Horeb and the burning bush because he realizes that one of the lambs he is shepherding has separated from the flock and will not survive on his own. He walks a long distance until he finds that little lamb drinking at a brook. Moses picks up the lost lamb and holds him in his arms until they both return to the flock. When God sees this act of compassion toward the lamb, the Midrash concludes, He knows He can trust Moses to be the liberator and lawgiver of the Israelites and all humans.

As God trusted Abraham and Moses, so then do the scriptures in turn call on us repeatedly and movingly to trust in God.

> "*Trust* [emphasis added] in the Lord with all your heart… In all your ways acknowledge him, and he will make straight your paths" (Proverbs 3:5 ESV).

> "Blessed is the one who *trusts* [emphasis added] in the Lord, whose confidence is in Him. They will be like a tree planted by the water that sends out its roots by the stream" (Jeremiah 17:7–8 NIV).

> "For we live by faith, not by sight" (2 Corinthians 5:7 NIV). In other words, we live by trusting God.

> "*Trust* [emphasis added] in the Lord and
> do good; dwell in the land and enjoy safe
> pasture" (Psalm 37:3 NIV).

Our trust in God is at the heart of our faith in God, but trust is also different from faith. Faith is the belief that God exists. Trust is the confidence that God will do what He has promised if we do what He asks of us. That kind of trust in each other is exactly what our political leaders and the rest of us need now to reunite America.

One more thought about trust in politics.

In my personal and political life, I have noted that people tend to trust people of faith because they believe the faithful live and act in awe or fear of God. That is not always true, of course, but most religious people do feel accountable to God for their behavior, and others therefore trust them unless they show by their actions that their faith does not really guide their behavior and they don't deserve to be trusted. Remember George Washington's warning that a democracy cannot be moral without the presence of faith among its leaders and people.

When I was a child, my maternal grandmother, who had emigrated from Romania to America, told me that she had been taught by her parents in Europe that if she were to ever be in a taxi (probably horse-drawn in those days) driven by a Christian man, and it went by a church and he did not cross himself, she should immediately get out of the taxi, because she could not *trust* that driver to do the right thing.

Senator Joe Lieberman

At times in my own career, I felt that I benefited from such trust because I was known to be religiously observant. That made me work hard to justify that trust. This suggests that people in politics who are religious might give their colleagues the confidence to trust them more if they let those colleagues know that the ethics of their faith guide their conduct.

> It is better to take refuge in the Lord than
> to trust in man. (Psalm 118:8 ESV)

We are, of course, justified in having greater confidence in God than in our fellow humans, and yet if we are unable to trust in man, as is too often the case in politics and government today, we will not be able to make the kind of humanitarian and moral progress that God wants us to. That is why the goals of eliminating extreme partisanship and restoring civility are aimed at rebuilding trust. This trust will enable us to once again have respectful debates and will lead to constructive compromises that get good things done for our country.

CHAPTER SIX

The Demise of Debate

America's founders had great debates at the Constitutional Convention before they could reach an agreement on the documents that would make the states a nation. There were serious disagreements among them about important issues, such as how the thirteen states would be represented in Congress and what to say about slavery. The delegates understood that it was mandatory to debate their differences on and off the convention floor if they were to find their way to compromises that would enable their new nation to begin. The debates were vigorous but respectful. Some of their compromises were brilliant (as with representation in Congress) and some were horrible (as with slavery). But in the end, they succeeded in producing a constitution that was ratified, and the rest is American history.

Our Founding Fathers believed that good debates would always be necessary to sustain and strengthen the democratic republic the Constitution created. On the marble wall at the Jefferson Monument in Washington, the following words of our third president are written:

> Truth is…the proper antagonist to error,
> and has nothing to fear from the conflict
> unless by human interposition disarmed
> of her natural weapons: free argument
> and debate.

In the United States, we believe that free argument and debate lead to truth and progress in politics and government, just as we believe free argument and debate in our courts lead to justice. Our history tells us that good debates also lead to compromises that solve problems and achieve progress. Such debates are a means of holding the government accountable to the governed and of educating the citizenry about the challenges of their time, so they can be informed when they vote.

Sadly, there are rarely good debates in American politics anymore. In fact, there are rarely *any* debates anymore, even in the required public "debates" in political campaigns. Those events have mostly become separate pronouncements of prepared talking points and one-liners by each candidate that produce more heat than light. Political discussions about the issues of the day, whether in public settings or in legislative chambers, are no longer really debates in the traditional meaning of the word—a discussion between people in which they express different opinions about a topic, and question each other.

In today's "debates," people generally don't engage with each other, question each other, or even recognize each other. They speak to the cameras or the crowds. There is no "free argument and debate," in Jefferson's words, that can lead to truth and progress. When you are propounding your opinion on a topic in the absence of others who take a different position and might challenge you or limit you if they were there, you are likely to be harsher and maybe even deceitful.

Civility has been forgotten. Personal slander has increased, and trust among our leaders has decreased. In my twenty-four years in the US Senate—the legislature that was once deserving of the title "the greatest deliberative body in the world"—genuine debates with respectful back-and-forth exchanges were the exception. When I first arrived, I was surprised by how little real debate among senators occurred. Even on big issues, such as the question in 1991 of whether Congress should authorize President Bush to take military action against Iraq in Kuwait, the debate was not a debate. It was a series of separate speeches by the senators to a largely empty chamber, but the television cameras were on and the media gallery was crowded.

The vision of our founders—that good debates in Congress not only would lead to good legislative results but would educate the public—is gone. Most of what the public learns about the important issues in America comes not from congressional debates but from slash-and-burn commercials during campaigns and, in between campaigns, from increasingly partisan media.

The best memories I have of any debate-like exchanges on the Senate floor were with John McCain, and they were not debates according to the traditional definition. They were colloquies—conversations between John and me. One would usually begin when one of us had seen something in the news that concerned or agitated us, and that person would call the other and say, "Did you see what Putin did yesterday?" or "…what the Taliban did?" or "…what the military government in Myanmar did?" This was followed by: "Let's go out to the floor and have a colloquy." That meant we would each speak, respond, and question each other for as long as we had something to say, or until another senator wanted to claim the floor. While those colloquies were not traditional debates, they were intellectually challenging for John and me and hopefully informative and thought-provoking for anyone who was watching.

The demise of good debates in American politics and government is not just the *result* of the partisanship, incivility, and distrust that dominate today; it has also become a *cause* of those corrosive behaviors.

Faith's Answers to America's Political Crisis

Here too the Bible has a lot to teach politicians, elected officials, and people in the media about the importance of good, honest, civil debates. The first great debate in the Bible is the surprising exchange between God and Abraham about the fate of the sinful people of Sodom and Gomorrah. It is surprising because of the courage and confidence Abraham had to dare to debate with the Almighty. Before that, God had reached the conclusion that He trusted Abraham enough to tell him what he intended to do to Sodom and Gomorrah. That divine trust opened up the door to the debate that followed, just as the restoration of trust among our leaders can lead to more constructive debates among them. In these words from Genesis (18:17–19 NKJV), God explains why He can trust Abraham enough to tell him He plans to destroy Sodom and Gomorrah, and thereby seems to be inviting Abraham's response:

> And the Lord said, "Shall I hide from Abraham what I am doing, since Abraham shall surely become a great and mighty nation, and all the nations of the earth shall be blessed in him? For I have known him, in order that he may command his children and his household after him, that they keep the way of the Lord, to do righteousness and justice."

And then, the Bible continues, Abraham "drew near" to the Lord and said:

> Wilt Thou indeed sweep away the righteous with the wicked...shall not the judge of all the earth do justly? (JPS)

The Lord responds to Abraham's argument against collective guilt:

> If I find in Sodom fifty righteous within the city, I will forgive all the place for their sake.

But Abraham is not finished. He continues with humility and respect:

> Behold now I have taken upon me to speak unto the Lord, though I am but dust and ashes. Peradventure, there shall lack five of the fifty righteous; wilt thou destroy all the city for lack of five?

And in a remarkable and memorable exchange, God lowers his demand to forty-five people. The debate and negotiations continue until God says:

> "I will not destroy it for the ten's sake."
> And the Lord went His way, as soon as

> He had left off speaking to Abraham; and
> Abraham returned to his place.

Moses had a similar debate with God after God said He would destroy the Israelites because they built the golden calf. And again, God relented in response to Moses' arguments. To me, these two debates Abraham and Moses had with God are extraordinarily powerful, heart-changing lessons about the opportunities provided by good debates that are based on good values between people who trust each other.

The New Testament has some excellent examples of good debates that emerge from people asking Jesus challenging questions:

> One of the teachers of the law came and
> heard them debating. Noticing that Jesus
> had given them a good answer, he asked
> him, "Of all the commandments, which
> is the most important?"
>
> "The most important one," answered
> Jesus, "is this. 'Hear, O Israel: The Lord
> our God, the Lord is one....'
>
> The second is this: 'Love your neighbor
> as yourself.' There is no commandment
> greater than these." (Mark 12:30–31
> NIV)

In Islam, good debate is valued, but excessive debate that can become a divisive quarrel is not.

> The Messenger of Allah said: "Whoever gives up telling lies in support of a false claim, a palace will be built for him in the outskirts of Paradise. Whoever gives up argument when he is right, a palace will be built for him in the middle [of Paradise]." (Sunan ibn Majah 51)

This same method of asking questions, providing answers, and having debates was used by Jewish scholars and rabbis after the destruction of the Second Temple in 70 CE forced the Jews into exile, and it was eventually codified and written down in the Talmud—the compilation of Jewish law that still governs Jewish religious life, and is still being debated in synagogues and study halls throughout the world.

The Talmud has been correctly described as "a sacred book of debates." It records not just the consensus resolution of the debates about religious laws but the arguments that were made and challenged along the way. The essence and importance of these debates are captured in a famous and poignant story recorded as a lesson in the Talmud itself about Rabbi Yohanan, who was the head of one of the great Talmudic schools, and his learned and distinguished colleague and study partner Rabbi Lakish.

Faith's Answers to America's Political Crisis

Rabbi Lakish died, and Rabbi Yohanan deeply mourned him. His students worried about Rabbi Yohanan and brought another leading scholar, Rabbi Elazar, to study with him. But when Rabbi Yohanan propounded a dictum, Rabbi Elazar would say, "There is a teaching which supports you." That irritated Rabbi Yohanan greatly, and he complained to Rabbi Elazar:

> When I stated a law, Rabbi Lakish used to raise twenty-four objections to which I gave twenty-four answers which consequently led to a fuller comprehension of the law; while all you do is offer arguments that support my opinion which I already know. (Bava Metzia 84a)

A more modern example of the value of debating and questioning one another is Isidor Rabi, the great American physicist who won the Nobel Prize and was a leader of the Manhattan Project during World War II. When asked why he had become such a great scientist, Rabi gave the credit to his Jewish mother: "When I came home from school, she would never ask me, 'What did you learn today?' Only, 'Issy, did you ask a good question?'"

The Talmud also tells a story of a dispute over religious law between the rival religious schools of Rabbi Hillel and Rabbi Shammai that instructs us how to debate. When the debate has ended:

...a voice issued from heaven announcing: "The teachings of both are the words of the living God, but the law is in agreement with the School of Hillel."

But [it was asked] since both are the words of the living God, for what reason was the School of Hillel entitled to have the law determined according to their rulings?

Because they were kindly and humble, and because they studied their own rulings and those of the School of Shammai, and even mentioned the teachings of the School of Shammai before their own. (Babylonian Talmud, Eruvin 13b)

The thoughtful and respectful way the proponents of the School of Hillel debated made it more likely that their conclusions would be truthful and just. Implicit in these words from the Talmud is that Hillel's students might even say when they thought the School of Shammai had made a good point because they had listened to the Shammai students' arguments and had thought seriously about them.

These lessons from our religious texts about the importance of good debates in achieving good results are far from today's political discourse. But they are not beyond the reach and capacities of our political leaders (and the media that report on them) if they want to get some good things done for our country and their constituents and not just do anything they can to win the next election or raise their ratings.

CHAPTER SEVEN

The Unwillingness to Compromise

Abraham Ribicoff was elected governor of Connecticut twice and then, for three terms, US senator from the state. For me, he was first a hero and then a valued mentor. When Abe—a Democrat—was elected governor, both houses of the Connecticut General Assembly had Republican majorities. He dealt with that political reality in his opening speech to the legislature, which he titled "The Integrity of Compromise." In it, he said that he and the Republicans could fight each other from behind their respective party lines for the next two years and get nothing done, or they could work together for the people who had elected them. They chose the latter and accomplished a lot.

"The Integrity of Compromise" was a brilliant title for that speech. In addition to publicly challenging the Republicans to work with him, by using the word *integrity* he was arguing that there is nothing wrong with compromise in politics. It is nothing to feel defensive or embarrassed about. Compromise has integrity. It is honorable. In fact, as Abe Ribicoff knew well, compromise is absolutely necessary in a democracy. Without compromise between different parties or factions in democratic politics and government, little or nothing will get done. That is what American history teaches us and what is painfully obvious these days from the inability of our elected representatives in Washington to take action together to deal with some of our major problems, including the enormous federal debt; the exciting but, to many, threatening technological changes of our time; immigration and border security; and the rapid changes in our societal cultural norms, which are thrilling but offensive to some.

All the problems in our politics today that we have discussed here, including extreme partisanship, incivility, distrust, and the absence of real debates, have led to an unwillingness to compromise. If we cannot work our way back to making compromise the rule and not the exception, our democracy will lose its legitimacy and our country will inevitably decline.

Compromise has been necessary since the founding of our republic, beginning with the convention in Philadelphia in 1787 that produced the Constitution. Difficult compromises were required to get enough votes for the document's passage in the convention and ratification by the people in the states. One of the most contentious issues in Philadelphia was how the states would be represented in the new Congress. The large-population states (led by Virginia) argued that representation should be based on population, while the smaller-population states (led by New Jersey) argued for equal representation for each state. The debates on this question were intense. Neither side was moving; today we would call it "gridlock." It was so bad that the delegates thought it best during the summer of 1787 to adjourn the convention. Many worried it would never reconvene. But negotiations among some of the delegates continued, and two of them from Connecticut—Roger Sherman and Oliver Ellsworth—proposed what became known in our history as the Great Compromise.

The new Congress would have not just one chamber, as had been assumed, but two. In one, the House, representation would be based on population. In the other, the Senate, each state would have two members. This compromise had a simple and wise logic to it that broke the gridlock. The convention reconvened, and the Constitution was adopted.

On more than one occasion during my time in the Senate, when negotiations on an important issue had broken off and the necessary compromises seemed out of reach, I would go to the Senate floor and retell the story of the Great Compromise (which I often proudly called the Connecticut Compromise, because its two proponents were from my state). I would challenge my colleagues, saying:

"Surely if this Senate in which we are privileged to serve was created by a compromise, we can find a way to compromise on the legislation before us."

Throughout American history, the two parties in Congress have achieved great things by compromising with each other. In the US Senate, compromise has been more imperative than it has been in the House because of the cloture rule requiring sixty votes to end a filibuster, and the political reality that it is rare for one party to elect sixty members. Examples of important legislation adopted with bipartisan support based on compromise are thankfully more recent than the Constitutional Convention of 1787. Here are some excellent and encouraging examples in America's modern history: the post–Second World War bipartisan legislative agreements on foreign and defense policy negotiated by President Truman and Arthur Vandenberg, the Republican chair of the Senate Foreign Relations Committee; the Civil Rights Act of 1960, which was enacted primarily because of agreements between President Johnson and Everett Dirksen, the Republican leader of the Senate; the compromises worked out by President Reagan and the Democratic House speaker, Tip O'Neil, during the 1980s, which secured (many would say saved) Social Security; and the agreements negotiated in 1997 by President Clinton and Newt Gingrich, the Republican speaker, by which bipartisan majorities in both chambers passed the Balanced Budget Act, which actually balanced the federal budget for the next three years—the last time that has happened.

In my years in the Senate, almost all of the accomplishments I feel best about resulted from bipartisan partnerships and compromises. They were diverse and included the Clean Air Act of 1990; the resolution authorizing military action to get Iraq out of Kuwait in 1991; the bipartisan congressional pressure on the White House to lead NATO into Bosnia to stop the aggression and genocide there during the early 1990s; the Balanced Budget Act of 1997; the creation of the Department of Homeland Security after 9/11; the comprehensive reform of our intelligence agencies as recommended by the bipartisan 9/11 Commission; the adoption of the American Resource and Recovery Act of 2009 to help the US recover from the financial collapse of 2008; and the repeal of the discriminatory "Don't Ask, Don't Tell" law in 2010.

In 2009, for a short while, there were sixty Democrats in the hundred-member Senate. The Obama administration, in its drive to enact health care reform that year, learned that to get the sixty votes needed for a bill to pass in the Senate, it had to negotiate compromises inside the Democratic caucus—since all the Republicans said they would oppose the bill. And negotiate was exactly what Rahm Emanuel, then chief of staff to the president, did with Democratic senators Ben Nelson of Nebraska, Mary Landrieu of Louisiana, Mark Pryor and Blanche Lincoln of Arkansas, and me.

In the end, after a fair amount of give-and-take, President Obama got the support of all sixty Democrats, and a very humane and transformational health care reform law was enacted. That goal had eluded presidents since Truman.

This record of great accomplishments that resulted from negotiations and compromises between both parties and sometimes within one party should be enough to motivate presidents and members of Congress to negotiate more such compromises today. The satisfaction is great, much greater than politicians would get by refusing to compromise to improve the odds that they and their party could win the next election.

In fact, some of the people who suffer most from the extreme partisanship and refusal to compromise that characterizes our government in Washington may be the members of Congress themselves. They work hard to get elected so they can make a difference for the better for their country and constituents, and then when they get to Washington, they allow themselves to be herded into warring partisan tribes and end up achieving little or nothing. Many of them are not happy in their work. That should motivate more bipartisan compromises that produce results, but it certainly has not done that yet.

Maybe if elected officials in Washington were to think more about how their religions encourage them to compromise, they would be empowered to liberate themselves from the stifling divisive grips of their political party and interest groups. To me, the most direct religious reasons to overcome extreme partisanship and the failure to compromise are the appeals of our religions to work for peace wherever we can. The most well-known and therefore the most important of these appeals is Jesus' Seventh Beatitude:

> Blessed are the peacemakers, for they will
> be called children of God. (Matthew 5:9
> NIV)

When many people read those words, the political division and dysfunction in our national government may not be the first conflicts that come to mind. But it is clear from the theological context and commentaries on the Seventh Beatitude that it does not just mean making peace between people at war. More frequently, it relates to differences of opinion among people that lead to serious conflicts, disunity, and hatred. If we think about all the negative results of the failure of our elected officials to compromise with each other to help our country and its people, anyone who can be an effective peacemaker deserves to be blessed, and even reelected.

The second part of the Seventh Beatitude makes a very important point that strengthens the call to make peace. Peacemakers are to be blessed "for they will be called children of God." To me, this means that as children of God, we understand that the people we disagree with about particular governmental policies are not enemies or aliens. They are fellow children of God, each with the spirit of God in them and therefore deserving of our respect and an effort to compromise with them for the common good. That understanding surely should make governmental mediation and peacemaking easier and more likely to succeed.

The second meaning of that second beatitude clause is also very important. All religions encourage their followers to take God's behavior, as described in religious texts, as a norm to try to emulate here on Earth. In this case, when I read that peacemakers will be called children of God, it means that when we strive to end conflict among people and, in political terms, find common ground, we are emulating the God of peace. We are doing the Lord's work. It makes clear that we understand our responsibility as children of God.

The Bible contains several examples of conflicts that are peacefully resolved through compromise that we can learn from. For example, in Numbers, nearly forty years after the Exodus, when the Israelites are close to the Promised Land, God directs Moses and the high priest, Elazar, to take a census of the Israelites and then divide the land among the various tribes, their leaders, and the sons of their leaders.

But the five daughters of Zelophehad, who was a descendant of Joseph, feel they have been treated unfairly and draw near to Moses and Elazar. They remind the two men that their father died in the wilderness without any male heirs. Now his daughters ask, "Why should the name of our father be done away from among his family, because he hath no son? Give unto us *therefore* a possession among the brethren of our father" (Numbers 27:4 KJV).

Moses is moved by their appeal and brings "their cause before the Lord," who responds to Moses: "The daughters of Zelophehad speak right: thou shalt surely give them a possession of an inheritance among their father's brethren [members of his tribe]; and thou shalt cause the inheritance of their father to pass unto them" (Numbers 27:7 KJV). That is a wonderful, divinely ordained compromise. The daughters inherit the land that would have been given to their father if he were alive, but it must be kept within his tribe of Menashe.

The leading figures in the Bible also were peacemakers who negotiated compromises that avoided larger conflicts. For example, in Genesis 13, after Abraham and Lot and their families leave Egypt and settle in Beth El in Israel, they find that the land for grazing around Beth El cannot sustain the large number of cattle they all now have.

"And there was a strife between the herdsman of Abram's cattle and the herdsmen of Lot's cattle," the Bible tells us. Then Abraham steps in and offers a generous compromise to end the conflict. He says to Lot:

> Let there be no strife, I pray thee, between
> me and thee, and between my herdmen
> and thy herdmen; for we are brethren. Is

> not the whole land before thee? Separate
> thyself, I pray thee, from me; if thou wilt
> take the left hand, then I will go to the
> right; or if thou take the right hand, then
> I will go to the left. (JPS)

Lot chooses the plain of Jordan to the east, and Abraham chooses the land of Canaan to the west.

I have chosen these two examples of compromise from the Bible because the conflicts they settled are so realistic and, in ways, ordinary, and because the compromises are so balanced and fair—just like the ones that are needed in our national government.

Other religious texts and teachers also appeal for peace through compromise. For example:

> If two parties…fall into a quarrel, make
> peace between them…with justice and
> be fair. (Quran 49:9)

The quest for tranquility and peace, including through compromise, is also at the heart of the Hindu religion.

The imperative to compromise has often been linked to appeals to live by the golden mean, which is a natural way to achieve a fair compromise. The twelfth-century Spanish-Jewish scholar, philosopher, and doctor Maimonides wrote: "The right way is the mean…namely that disposition that is equally distant from the two extremes in its class."

The same lesson is prominent in Christian texts and teachings:

> Let your moderation be known unto all men [because] the Lord is at hand. (Philippians 4:5 KJV)

St. Thomas Aquinas wrote in his *Summa Theologica*:

> Evil consists in discordance from the rule of measure or...falling short of it. Therefore, it is evident that moral virtue observes the mean.

John Calvin declared in his *Institutes of the Christian Religion* that:

> There is no kind of government more salutary than one in which liberty is properly exercised with becoming moderation...

He added:

> The purpose of political government and law is to cultivate civil restraint and righteousness in people, and to promote general peace and liberty.

The philosophers of the Enlightenment in the eighteenth century also supported moderation and compromise in a way that was quite consistent with the Judeo-Christian teachings that the first American leaders knew so well. In his treatise "The Spirit of Law," for example, Montesquieu wrote that the essence of his political philosophy was "the spirit of moderation."

During my years as a lawmaker, one of the appeals for compromise I heard most frequently was that "the perfect is the enemy of the good." I long assumed these words had first been spoken by an early-twentieth-century American political boss. I later learned they were written by Voltaire, a philosopher of the Enlightenment. His words are wise and realistic, particularly in a democracy like ours. If elected officials demand perfection, they will achieve nothing. If they compromise, they can do much that is good.

My prayer is that our elected representatives in Washington, and the people who own and operate the media that report on them, will stop dividing themselves and us by refusing to compromise or refusing to report on compromises favorably. Instead they should start reaching out to each other for the unity and truth that produce progress and solutions to our problems. They can and should become makers of peace, remembering the blessing that will come to those who do:

> Blessed are the peacemakers, for they shall be called children of God. (Matthew 5:9 NIV)

CHAPTER EIGHT

Do We Really Need Governments?

The question of whether people need government seems ridiculously unnecessary. We all know the answer: "Of course we need government, to do for us what we cannot do for ourselves." But one of the worst consequences of the current partisanship in our politics and the disability of our government is the large number of Americans whose opinions of the US government are so negative and whose distrust and anger toward our government is so great that many of them seem to be asking whether we would be better off without a government at all.

Americans have always had a healthy (often humorous) skepticism toward government and politicians. For evidence of that, I refer you to Mark Twain, Will Rogers, or any of the current late-night television comedians. But these days, if you listen to talk radio, follow social media, or watch cable television, you will hear deadly serious anger, fury, and even threats of violence toward the government and the public servants who run it that leave Twain and Rogers not just decades behind but worlds away.

The January 6, 2021, attack on the US Capitol and on our elected representatives who were in it was an attack on the "citadel" of the democratic republic created by the Constitution. I have chosen the word *citadel* intentionally. In scripture, God protects the citadels of Jerusalem (Psalm 48:4–14), which are described as the citadels in which the righteous find safety (Proverbs 18:10).

To me, the destruction and desecration of the Capitol on January 6, 2021, and the threats that day to hang the vice president of the United States and kill the speaker of the House went beyond opposition to the results of the election and anger toward our government. They were acts of anarchy—attacks on government itself, a rebellion against our government as we have known it and a mindless appeal for a country without a government.

Governments are created by people, because people need a central authority to, at a minimum, protect them from external enemies and threats, to establish and enforce rules of behavior that are good for the community, and to provide services for people who are in need. All these are functions that individuals cannot perform for themselves, and so over history, people have formed governments out of necessity to perform them.

> Pray for the welfare of the government,
> for were it not for the fear of it, people
> would swallow each other alive. (Talmud,
> Ethics of the Fathers 3:2)

In the Bible, the first evidence that God wants us to govern ourselves and to do so according to values (ultimately in law) comes in Genesis 2:15, when He directs Adam and Eve to "work and guard" (some translations say "enjoy and protect") all the glorious and beautiful creations He has made and placed in the Garden of Eden. In other words, God wanted Adam and Eve to take pleasure and make progress from His creations but also charged them with a responsibility to protect those creations, presumably for future generations. This divine directive could be thought of as history's first executive order, and eventually as the basis for modern environmental conservation and protection laws and regulations.

From Abraham to Joseph in the Bible, the Israelites were a growing family that lived under foreign governments. In Egypt, they grew to number more than two million. When God and Moses liberated them from slavery and led them to Mount Sinai, Moses himself became their first real form of self-government, because they were free and needed one. They would not survive if each of them did whatever they wanted.

Moses held all the powers of government—executive, legislative, and judicial—until his wife's father, Jethro, intervened and convinced Moses to delegate authority and responsibility and thereby begin a government:

> Select capable men from all the people—
> men who fear God, trustworthy men
> who hate dishonest gain.... Have them
> serve as judges for the people at all times,
> but have them bring every difficult case
> to you; the simple cases they can decide
> themselves. (Exodus 18:21–22 NIV)

In Numbers 11:16–17, God directs Moses to develop an even broader government with greater powers:

> Bring me seventy of the leaders of Isra'el,
> people you recognize as leaders of the
> people and officers of theirs. Bring them
> to the tent of meeting, and have them
> stand there with you. I will come down
> and speak with you there, and I will take
> some of the Spirit which rests on you and
> put it on them. Then they will carry the
> burden of the people along with you, so
> that you won't carry it yourself alone.
> (CJB)

The Sanhedrin, or supreme court, that emerged in later Jewish history had seventy-one members representing the original seventy elders and Moses, ordained in the Bible. And it had a combination of judicial and legislative powers. The executive power was eventually exercised by the judges and kings. "When you come to the land that the Lord your God is giving you," Moses says in Deuteronomy (17:14–15 ESV), "and then say, 'I will set a king over me, like all the nations that are around me,' you may indeed set a king over you whom the Lord your God will choose." The Israelites were given the right to have a king rule over them, but only one who was chosen by God and understood that his power as king was dependent on God and had to be exercised according to the laws in God's Bible:

> When he takes the throne of his kingdom, he is to write for himself on a scroll a copy of this law, taken from that of the Levitical priests. It is to be with him, and he is to read it all the days of his life so that he may learn to revere the Lord his God and follow carefully all the words of this law and these decrees (Deuteronomy 17:18–19 NIV)

The Mishnah of the later rabbinical period expanded the king's required personal connection to the Bible:

> And he shall write a Bible in his own name. When he goes forth to war, he

must take it with him; on returning he
brings it back with him: when he sits in
judgment, it shall be with him. (Sanhedrin 2:4)

In Chapter 8 of the Book of Samuel, the people demand a king as predicted. Samuel chooses Saul and imposes on the new king strong rules of compliance with God's will.

This same section of Deuteronomy that authorizes kings contains one of the most important sentences in the Bible. It must be connected to everything else said about the necessity and nature of government:

Justice, justice shall you pursue. (Deuteronomy 16:20)

The Bible is saying here that government—in this first case, a monarchy—is needed by people for their own good, including the prevention and punishment of crime and the resolution of civil disputes, but that government must always pursue and protect justice in ways that are just. The noble end of justice can never be achieved and protected by unjust means.

Similar arguments for and about government are fundamental to the other Abrahamic faiths. When Jesus is asked whether it is right to pay taxes to the pagan government of Caesar, he answers famously:

> Give back to Caesar what is Caesar's and
> to God what is God's. (Matthew 22:15–
> 22 NIV)

According to Romans (13:4 NKJV), government is "God's minister, an avenger to *execute* wrath on him who practices evil." Therefore, people must not seek revenge themselves. God will see that justice is done, and earthly governments are one of God's ways to do that (Romans 12:17–19).

> "We must obey God rather than men,"
> said Peter. (Acts 5:29 ESV)

But elsewhere, Peter adds a fuller balancing of the roles of God and government:

> Be subject for the Lord's sake to every
> human institution, whether it be to the
> emperor as supreme, or to governors as
> sent by him to punish those who do evil
> and to praise those who do good…. Live
> as people who are free…as servants of
> God. (1 Peter 2:13–17 ESV)

And from Timothy comes an invocation to pray for the government to do good:

> I urge that supplications, prayers, inter-
> cessions, and thanksgivings be made…

for kings and all who are in high positions, that we may lead a peaceful and
quiet life, godly and dignified in every
way. (1 Timothy 2:1–2 ESV)

These words are very similar to those of Jeremiah (29:7
NIV) to the Israelites in exile in Babylonia:

Seek the peace and prosperity of the city
to which I have carried you into exile.
Pray to the LORD for it, because if it
prospers, you too will prosper.

In Islam, there is also a rich body of precedent that
argues for the necessity of good governments to carry out
God's will and values on Earth. The Quran tells us what
a government guided by the tenets of Islam should be. In
the year 622, the Prophet moved from Mecca to Yathrib.
For ten years, he was both the religious and political leader
of the growing Muslim community there and in Medina.
From that position of centralized power, he negotiated and
implemented what might be called the Compact of Medina,
an impressively democratic agreement that embraced and
balanced the values of religion and governance. It did not
create an exclusively Muslim state but was based on the religious values that had been revealed to Muhammad and
that the scribes had recorded in the Quran. Before it could
be implemented, the Prophet required the consent of all the
citizens—Muslim and non-Muslim.

Therefore, the first Islamic State was a constitutional democracy! Its main policy goal, as stated repeatedly in the Quran, was to create a society of peace and security in which every person could develop their physical, mental, and spiritual potential. The Arabic word for this is *falah*, which means realizing within ourselves the potential that Allah, the Creator, has put in each of us.

For long periods of Jewish history, when the Israelites were in exile from the Holy Land and therefore could not exercise sovereign governmental authority over themselves, the practical principle of governance that guided them as citizens of other countries is found in the Talmud (Avot 3:2):

> The law of the land [or the government
> under which you are living] is the law.

In other words, the civil and criminal laws of the country in which they lived were binding on the Jewish residents of the land with the authority of Jewish religious law. Violations of the laws of the land would be considered violations of Jewish religious law. There were three conditions for this respect of national laws: First, the foreign government must be legitimate; second, the law in question must apply to Jewish and non-Jewish residents alike; and third, the law must not conflict with the laws of the Bible.

Since the establishment of the modern state of Israel in 1948 and the reality of renewed Jewish sovereignty over the Holy Land, modern courts have been established that aim to integrate the history of Jewish governance and law, beginning in the Bible, with the modern realities of Israeli statehood and law, all under the primary guidance from Deuteronomy (16:20 CJB): "Justice, only justice, you must pursue."

The extraordinary way America's founders based their new government on faith in God and on the lessons they had learned from the Judeo-Christian tradition sustained them to victory through the most difficult days of the war for independence and enabled them to maintain national unity during the early, challenging decades of American history.

That unity and shared sense of national purpose have prevailed during most of American history.

But not now. Now the American people's trust and confidence in our government and its elected leaders have collapsed. The people are not just angry to the point of anarchy. They are more broadly pessimistic than ever before about our future, and that represents a separate, serious, self-fulfilling threat to America. At least two-thirds of the people consistently say they think America is going in the wrong direction.[2] We know from our own lives that being optimistic about the future motivates people to act to make the future better. There are other reasons people might

2   In an Associated Press/NORC Research Center Poll released on October 14, 2023, 78 percent of respondents said they believed America was headed in the wrong direction.

have for their current pessimism than the dismal state of our governance, including rapid technological changes that will leave a lot of people behind, and changes in the natural world that have caused so many catastrophes and threaten to cause many more. But it is hard to dispute that major causes of America's dark mood are the overall fecklessness of our government and the resulting conclusion that it cannot deal effectively with any big changes or challenges.

That is why we all need to remind ourselves of the answer to the seemingly unnecessary question I asked at the beginning of this chapter. Yes, we definitely do need government. We need America's government to be much better than it has been. We the people and those we elect to lead our government have the power to make it so. They and we urgently must.

CHAPTER NINE

Have the Partisanship and Division in Our Politics and Government Mattered to Our Legal System?

Has the crisis in our politics affected our legal system? Unfortunately, it has. Article 3 of the Constitution established a system of federal courts that are intended to be independent and above partisan politics. But today they are not, and that is a profound threat to our country. When the people respect and trust our courts as being independent and fair, they will accept the courts' final judgments, even when those judgments are not what they were hoping for. When the people suspect that the courts are partisan and unfair, our country is in real danger.

Opinions toward our highest court—the US Supreme Court—are in great decline and increasingly determined by whether a person is a Democrat or Republican, is liberal or conservative, is pro-choice or pro-life. Public trust in the Supreme Court is at its lowest and most partisan level ever, according to a Gallup poll taken in June 2023. Only 40 percent of the American people approved of the job the Supreme Court was doing—22 percent lower than in 2000, when Gallup first asked the question. Sixty-two percent of Republicans approved of the Supreme Court, but only 17 percent of Democrats did, a 45 percent partisan difference of opinion about what our founders wanted to be the least partisan of the three branches of our government.

Those differences of opinion about the Supreme Court are more than just interesting polling numbers. They threaten to deprive the court of its legitimacy, which in turn would soon significantly weaken the rule of law in America that has been so vital to every positive aspect of our society. If, notwithstanding all the legal rights given to people in America's legal system, large numbers of people refuse to accept its final judicial decisions, we are on the path to a society of lawlessness and chaos.

Former president Trump did great damage to the rule of law in America when he refused to accept the decisions against him in sixty of sixty-one lawsuits he filed to overturn the election of President Biden in 2020. Those sixty decisions against Trump were made by judges with a wide variety of legal philosophies who had been appointed by presidents and governors of both major political parties.

Faith's Answers to America's Political Crisis

The Talmud has a compelling—and literally fantastic—story that argues for respecting the final judgments of courts of law whether one agrees with them or not. Long ago, in a case before the Sanhedrin, the high court in Jerusalem, the majority of judges disagreed with their colleague Rabbi Eliezer. After every argument that he made failed to change the opinion of the other judges, he appealed to God for supernatural proof and support. Amazingly, trees uprooted themselves, streams reversed their flow, and a voice rang out from heaven supporting Rabbi Eliezer's argument.

But, even more amazingly, the other judges were not moved by such divine intervention. As one of them said, "The law is not in heaven." The opinion of the judge or a majority of judges here on Earth was final and must be respected. In a later text (Sefer HaChinuch, Mitzvah 496), this surprising decision was explained and defended:

> It is better to suffer what one believes is
> a mistake by a court, rather than have
> each individual act according to his own
> opinion, for that would cause…a divi-
> sion among the people and the complete
> loss of the nation.

Those words were written in Spain during the thirteenth century, but they argue compellingly against the threat that our American legal system faces in the twenty-first century because of the increasing refusal to accept final judicial judgments, and because of the growing public disrespect of courts and judges.

The surprisingly good news is that our legal system has held against all the challenges and partisan attacks associated with the 2020 election, including the violent attack on Congress in the US Capitol on January 6, 2021, which aimed to stop Congress from fulfilling its constitutional responsibility to count the electoral votes. Although the members of Congress were forced to leave the Capitol for a few hours to protect their lives on that dreadful day, they courageously returned before the day ended to finish their work. They provided for the peaceful transfer of power based on the validated election returns from the states. But there is no reason to assume that our rule-of-law system will survive other similar attacks on its legitimacy. We the people must act quickly and decisively to protect it.

For me, the most ominous evidence of the dangers we and our legal system now face are the threats on the lives of the nine Supreme Court justices, which have been deemed so real and so serious by law enforcement that each of the justices now has a security detail with him or her all day, every day. Equally troubling is the broad condemnation of the police, including appeals to defund them as a result of the misconduct of a small percentage of police in America. Without the police, who would enforce the law and protect us from criminals? Without courts that are respected, who will check and balance the police officers who are guilty of misconduct?

The importance that our religious faith and traditions attach to the law cries out against the current threats to America's legal system and to the police and judges who make it work. That religious perspective should remind us of how important the rule of law is to us, although we often take it for granted.

Not only do the law and courts punish and deter criminal behavior, but they also provide a nonviolent forum in which to settle civil disputes, including business disputes. In fact, the independence of our courts attracts both domestic and foreign businesses to invest in the US and create millions of jobs here. These businesses trust the American legal system to peacefully resolve any disagreements they might have and, at the extreme, to protect them from having their assets wantonly seized by our government.

In the moment when God gave Moses the Ten Commandments on Mount Sinai, the Israelites were transformed from a tribe to a legitimate nation. They had been given a code of rights and wrongs to guide them, and a national purpose, which was to live in observance of the Ten Commandments and to spread them to the rest of the world's people.

To be effective, a system of law must be credible and legitimate to the people (exactly the attributes our American system of law is now losing due to extreme partisanship).

The Ten Commandments are self-evidently and uniquely legitimate because they come from God. By asserting in the First Commandment that He brought the Israelites out of the Egyptian slave house, God is declaring that He is not only the God of Creation but also the God of history and justice, and that the Commandments that follow the first and second are *His* system of justice and therefore entitled to respect and observance. As I wrote earlier, the fact that I put one hand on a Bible every time I took an oath of public office, and that the oath always ended with the words "so help me God," reminded me that the basis of the legal system that I was swearing to uphold was God.

St. Thomas Aquinas taught that the Ten Commandments were a divine revelation. Because no individual can know the entire natural law, St. Thomas said, God revealed it in the Ten Commandments so it could be understood by all.

In the sixteenth century, Calvinism elevated the Ten Commandments and the Bible. It brought them into the laws of England, and then the Pilgrims brought them to America, where they inspired the Declaration of Independence and the Constitution. America's rule of law system was the result.

The Bible gives us a historical and philosophical context for God's giving of the law at Sinai that can help us understand the seriousness of the threat to our society from extreme partisanship, because of the importance of respect for the law in America. God's liberation of the Israelites from slavery in Egypt, as told in the Bible, was one of the most important and transformational events in human history. It expressed in action God's belief that freedom is the birthright of every one of His children, and that He would reenter history to protect that birthright.

But that was only the beginning of the story and the lessons from God. The Israelites were not emancipated to remain in Egypt or to live in the desert outside Egypt without a system of law.

The Exodus had a destination but also a purpose.

God's purpose in freeing the Israelites was to take them to Mount Sinai and give them and all of us the Ten Commandments—the laws that we should forever live by. In the biblical narrative that precedes Sinai, there was much to convince God that without a system of law, people would not survive for long: Adam and Eve could not obey the one directive that God gave them in the Garden of Eden; Cain killed Abel; Noah's generation was so sinful that God sent a great flood that killed everyone, leaving Noah and the animals he brought with him to begin history anew; and then God destroyed Sodom and Gomorrah because he could not find ten good people there.

By the time of the Exodus, there was more than enough evidence of the awful imperfection of people. They needed a system of laws to mandate and motivate their better natures and punish their bad behavior. They needed a system of law that came from God so that the "fear of Heaven" would lead them to observe those laws. In that broader understanding of the laws given at Sinai and the laws that have been enacted since, we codify our understanding of what is right and wrong, and express our aspirations for living better lives in a better community than we would be able to without the law.

That meaning of the law at Sinai and its profound importance to the human race ever since is now threatened in America every time someone refuses to accept the judgment of a court, or makes a partisan or ideological attack on the courts, judges, or police. If we do not stop such behavior, we will not survive as a nation. The faith-based rule of law in America is that important to us.

What can we do now to rebuild nonpartisan trust in our courts and legal system?

First, each of us must remind our fellow Americans that our legal system began at Sinai when God gave Moses the Ten Commandments. Attacks on it and the finality of its judgments and on the judges, police, and courts that implement the rule of law therefore not only will lead to chaos in our society but also are contrary to God's will.

Second, we need our political leaders and elected officials of both major political parties, the owners of the American media, and the leaders of every other sector in our society to defend the rule of law from partisan attacks. They must do this not just by counterattacking those in both major parties who are undermining the rule of law, but by explaining why the independence and fairness of our legal system mean so much to the security, freedom, and prosperity of every American.

Third, voters should not support any candidate for office who does not support the rule of law; an independent, non-partisan judiciary; and the police who are on the front lines of law and justice protecting the rest of us.

CHAPTER TEN

Does the Partisanship in Our Politics Affect America's Security in the World?

Partisan division in domestic American politics hurts our standing in the world. The reasons are obvious. When America is united at home, we are naturally stronger in the world. When we are divided, we are weaker and less able to protect our security, prosperity, and freedom. Our enemies are emboldened by our division. Our allies are unsettled by it and begin to look elsewhere for a different world power they can depend on.

The global war against Islamist terrorism that began on 9/11 is not over, as we saw in the barbaric terrorist attack by Hamas on Israeli citizens on October 7, 2023. In the United States, we have greatly improved our homeland security and intelligence capacities and coordination against terrorism

117

since 9/11. But now, we have entered a new chapter in world history in which the United States will be challenged and threatened by a powerful alliance of autocratic, aggressive governments in Russia, North Korea, China, and Iran. The extremist Islamist regime in Tehran, Iran, remains the world's foremost state sponsor of terrorism, both directly and through its agents in Hamas, Hezbollah, the Houthis, and the Shia militias in Syria and Iraq. I will call the four above-named countries the Axis of Dictators, four nations each governed by one person with absolute power.

We cannot weaken ourselves in meeting this next great challenge to our country and our way of life by letting mindless political partisanship divide us at home. To do that, we need to reconnect to all the lessons that our faith in God teaches us, so that we can stop the extreme partisanship of our politics. But we also need to go back and learn from difficult times in American history, when leaders of both major political parties came together to defend our security from foreign enemies and to uphold our national democratic values. In the past several decades, there has been no better, more instructive, and more inspiring bipartisan partnership than the one between Democratic president Harry Truman and Republican senator Arthur Vandenberg after the Second World War, at the beginning of the Cold War.

Arthur Vandenberg was a very conservative Republican from Michigan who was elected to the US Senate in 1928 and served until 1951, part of that time as chairman of the

Senate Foreign Relations Committee. During the 1930s, he opposed US involvement in the war and even urged President Roosevelt to seek an accommodation with the Japanese. He was an isolationist. But after the Japanese attack on Pearl Harbor, Vandenberg essentially said, "Anyone who remains an isolationist after Pearl Harbor is not a realist." So, he no longer was one.

After the war, as Republican chairman of the Foreign Relations Committee, Vandenberg began a bipartisan partnership with Truman in support of the great postwar international institutions and of strong new policies against the Soviet Union, including the Marshall Plan, the Truman Doctrine, and NATO.

In 1947, Vandenberg's Republican colleagues asked him to stop working so closely with Truman, because they hoped to defeat the Democrat in the 1948 presidential election. But Vandenberg resolutely and famously responded that "politics stop at the water's edge." He explained that he assumed there would always be differences of opinion about important foreign policy decisions, but that they should not be determined by party affiliation, because that would undermine America in the world and encourage our enemies to further divide us, and to think about attacking us or one of our allies.

The Vandenberg–Truman partnership during the postwar period and Vandenberg's defense of it remain the gold standard for bipartisan support of America's foreign policy.

Unfortunately, that standard has not been met very often since then, and fewer and fewer times in recent years as the partisanship in our domestic politics has grown worse and worse. That is one reason why our country's position in the world has diminished.

During my years in the Senate, there were some strong bipartisan partnerships in international crises—such as our bipartisan work to convince presidents from both major parties (Bush and Clinton) to stop the aggression and genocide in the Balkans, and the broad bipartisan support after the Soviet Union collapsed for quickly admitting the liberated nations of Eastern and Central Europe into NATO. But more frequently there were divisions of opinion on important foreign policy and national security decisions, and too many of those seemed to be determined by party affiliation rather than by the security interests of the US.

During the lead-up to the Gulf War of 1991, for example, I was troubled by the impression I had, based on statements I heard in Senate Democratic Caucuses, that some Democrats believed that if President Bush decided to go to war to get Iraq out of Kuwait, he should bear the political risks of his decision without Democratic support. That was putting politics and partisanship over national security.

On the other hand, after the catastrophic terrorist attacks of 9/11, our country and its elected leaders did come together. There was also bipartisan support in Congress for the war in Afghanistan to oust the Taliban government, which had been housing Osama bin Laden and Al-Qaeda while they planned their attacks on us. A few years later, there was similar bipartisan support in Congress for the war to overthrow Saddam Hussein in Iraq. But after our military toppled the Taliban and Saddam and the postwar situation in Afghanistan and Iraq got more difficult, partisan divisions reoccurred. Most Republicans argued that we should stay in both countries until they were stable and secure. I agreed, but most Democrats pushed for early withdrawal. On one vote in the Senate to cut off financial support to America's troops in Iraq, I was the deciding vote against the amendment and the only Democrat to vote that way.

It was understandable that some senators would think we should leave Iraq as quickly as possible, and that others would disagree. But it made no sense that all Republicans would vote one way and every Democrat besides me would vote the other way. Partisanship had taken over. Democrats wanted to hurt President Bush; Republicans wanted to protect him. And the national security interest of the United States took a back seat.

This type of partisanship must end. Our growing conflict with the Axis of Dictators has begun. Russia has invaded Ukraine and threatens other countries in Eastern and Central Europe. China threatens Taiwan and is massively building up its military in the Asia Pacific and beyond. Iran-backed Hamas has attacked Israel, and its militias have repeatedly attacked American troops stationed in the Middle

East. North Korea has been waving its nuclear swords and missiles, and threatens South Korea and Japan. All four of the dictatorial powers threaten the United States regularly.

This is no time for partisan politics at home to weaken either our defenses against the Axis of Dictators or our possible offensive actions against them. We must pull together in defense of America. We must put America first and forget about our political party affiliation in our international relations.

We must work our way back to the Truman–Vandenberg spirit in foreign policy, even if we can't yet end partisanship on domestic issues.

Partisan politics really must end at the nation's shores.

Are there ways in which the religious faith in God that most Americans and their elected leaders have can play a part in strengthening our foreign policy? There are—first by our remembering that the lessons of our faith should reduce or eliminate the incivility, distrust, absence of good debate, and unwillingness to compromise that create such partisan division in Washington and throughout America. The resulting American unity would definitely strengthen our position in the world against the terrorists and dictators.

But there is another unique and more substantive way our religious traditions can help strengthen our foreign policy. It is by bringing our national embrace of faith in God and our protection of religious freedom to the center of our foreign policy where they rightly belong, because those two principles are who we Americans are. And they are at the heart of our conflict with the Axis of Dictators.

The United States was established by and in faith. Our founders declared America's independence to secure the rights to life, liberty, and the pursuit of happiness that God, our creator, has endowed every person with. Article 6 of the Constitution prohibits religious tests for holding public office. That was a remarkably principled and selfless act by the men who wrote the Constitution. They were all Christians, and yet they chose to put a provision in the Constitution that would forever prohibit any attempt to deny Americans who are not Christians the ability to hold office in our country. The First Amendment to the Constitution enshrined religious liberty by guaranteeing freedom of religion to every American and prohibiting the establishment of any one religion by the government.

For millions of people of faith living in the shadows in the Axis of Dictators countries, our focus on faith will be very appealing as compared to the suppression of their faith by the governments under which they are forced to live. The fact that the US has from its creation been a faith-based country should lead us always to advance the values of faith in our public diplomacy. That means the values of democracy, the rule of law, and human rights that flow naturally from the Declaration and the Constitution. The endowment of rights from our creator was surely an endowment not just for Americans but for every person—every child of God—everywhere on Earth. That should be a rock on which American foreign policy goes forward—particularly now against Russia, China, Iran, and North Korea. History shows that we are always at our best in international relations when our foreign policy reflects our national values, so many of which come from our Judeo-Christian traditions.

The era of conflict we have entered with the Axis of Dictators will require us to remain strong in all elements of our national power, including military, economic, intelligence, cyber intelligence, and communications. But we can never forget that what underlies the confrontation between us and the dictators is our radically different national ideologies. The conflict between us is an ideological conflict. We and our allies are democracies. Russia, China, Iran, and North Korea are tyrannies. That difference is a big reason why the four of them are now allied against us, even though it would be much better for China to be allied with the US. We annoy China and the others when we protest and sanction their denial of the human rights of their citizens. We anger them when we oppose and deter their military aggression toward their neighbors. We are not like them, and they are not like us. Our faith-based national values are the opposite of the denial and corruption of those values in the Axis of Dictators.

China and North Korea are officially atheistic governments. Iran claims to be an Islamist religious state, and the Russians are mostly Orthodox Christians. But the governments of Russia and Iran most certainly do not respect the values of Christianity and Islam in their policies. The dictators who run those four countries understand that their struggle with us and our allies is about civilizational values. It is not just military or economic. We must understand that as well as they do. They believe our values are declining and theirs are rising. The political division they see (and stimulate when they can) in our country leads them to believe that we have lost our will to fight to the finish for the ideals that won two world wars and the Cold War. They think we have become morally soft and vulnerable, and they are not reluctant to say so: "The moral, historical truth is on our side," Russia's Vladimir Putin said in his 2023 New Year Address.

At the United Nations General Assembly in the fall of 2023, Ebrahim Raisi of Iran triumphantly declared: "The world is transitioning into a novel international order, and the project to Americanize the world has failed."

President Xi Jinping, in his speech to the Chinese Communist Party's Twentieth National Congress in 2022, said: "Scientific socialism is brimming with renewed vitality in twenty-first-century China. Chinese modernization offers humanity a new choice for achieving modernization."

That choice offered by Xi, Putin, Raisi, and North Korea's Kim Jong Un to their people and the world is a terrible one. It requires the people to give up their God-given human rights. That would not be the choice that most of the citizens in those countries and elsewhere would make if they had the freedom to choose. It is certainly not the choice America's founders made.

Shocking evidence of the ongoing denials of human rights and religious freedom by these four governments can be found in many places, one of the most credible of which are the reports of the International Religious Freedom Commission (IRFC), which was created by Congress in 1998 to help bring religious freedom into the center of our foreign policy. One of the best ways the commission is required and empowered to do that is with its annual report on the state of religious freedom in *every* country in the world, along with a requirement that those evaluations be used by the State Department in America's bilateral relations with each of the countries.

In its most recent report, the commission gave the four dictatorships we are focused on its worst rating, which means that the government of each has engaged in or tolerated "particularly severe violations of religious freedom, and those include torture, prolonged detention without charges, forced disappearance or other flagrant denial of life, liberty or security of people based on their religion."

The following are summaries of the commission's 2022 report on the Axis of Dictators countries:

> **China:** Religious freedom continued to deterio-
> rate. Religious people with alleged "foreign con-

nections"—such as Uyghurs and other Muslims, Tibetan Buddhists, and underground Catholics and Protestants—are especially vulnerable to persecution. Religious content has been banned from the internet. The commission report cites a finding by the UN Human Rights Commission that the forced labor of Uyghurs in Xinjiang "may amount to enslavement."

Iran: Following the death of twenty-two-year-old Iranian woman Mahsa Amini in 2022, after her arrest and torture by the so-called morality police for wearing an "improper" hijab, Iran suppressed widespread protests with lethal force, detained and killed children, and sexually assaulted, raped, and often executed protesters without any due process. The Iranian government also escalated its repression of members of the Baha'i faith, including restricting access by Baha'is to their communal religious sites. Iranian security forces destroyed a Sunni Muslim mosque and tortured a Sunni cleric to death. The government also sentenced a group of Iranian Christians to ten years in jail for their membership in a house church.

North Korea: The conditions of religious freedom are among the worst in the world. In North Korea, religion is considered a competing ideology to the government's and an existential threat. Therefore, the government aims to eliminate religions from the country and to severely punish the faithful. In North Korea, Christians are targets of persecution.

Russia: The Russian government increasingly prosecutes members of minority religious communities under a general law against extremist organizations. Many Jehovah's Witnesses have been detained, imprisoned, and fined under this law. Protestants, Catholics, and Muslims have been targeted as well. After Russia invaded Ukraine in February 2022, there were credible reports that Russian military personnel were torturing and "disappearing" Ukrainian religious leaders as a way of exerting control over local populations. In the first six months of the war, at least twenty Ukrainian religious figures were reportedly killed, and another fifteen were kidnapped. As of January 2024, UNESCO reported that at least 126 Ukrainian religious sites had been damaged by the Russian military.

These reports on religious persecution in the four Axis of Dictators countries illustrate how different the United States is from them. They also show how important it is for us and our allies always to stress those differences in religious freedom and faith-based values to the rest of the world, and to the people of these four countries, who suffer so much under their governments.

Our motto in a public diplomacy campaign to the people of Russia, China, Iran, and North Korea could be a variation on an old appeal that worked for Moses: "Let your people who want to serve God go to serve God."

And, while you're at it, let them enjoy all the human rights that are their endowment from our creator.

In his Inaugural Address in 1961, President Kennedy said:

> The world is very different now.... And yet the revolutionary beliefs for which our forefathers fought are still at issue around the globe—the belief that the rights of man come not from the generosity of the state but from the hand of God.

In the years ahead in our conflict with these four dictatorships, those revolutionary beliefs will be as much at issue as they were in the Cold War and in the American Revolution. We should remember that the original motto that Franklin, Jefferson, and Adams proposed for the United States was: "Rebellion to tyrants is obedience to God."

If we bring the forces of faith and religious freedom into the battle with the Axis of Dictators, along with our military and economic might, we will be as victorious in this next global challenge as our forebears were in the American Revolution and the Cold War.

CHAPTER ELEVEN

America Needs a Religious Awakening and a New Political Covenant

I asked a question at the beginning of this book that I have tried to answer in every chapter since: Can the faith in God held by most Americans, including most elected officials, help our country find its way out of the divisive and destructive political morass we have fallen into?

When I posed that question, I already thought that the answer would be positive. After writing this book, which has been a journey of research and reflection for me, I have firmly concluded that the faith that most Americans share can indeed help us return to national unity and a more effective government.

I have focused on the most important causes and effects of the political crisis America is in—partisanship, incivility, distrust, inability to debate, and unwillingness to compromise—and suggested ways that the values and lessons that flow from our faith can help us solve our political problems. Now the question is, *how* do we best bring those aspirational values of our religions into the battle to reform American politics? Praying to God can certainly motivate and strengthen us. But for the necessary changes to occur, we need to do more than pray. We need to have the faith to lead.

In Exodus 14 of the Bible, we find an inspirational role model for what we all need to do now. The liberation from Egyptian slavery has already happened, and the Israelites are at the Red Sea on their way to the Promised Land. Then the pharaoh's mighty army closes in on them. Their backs are to the water. They feel trapped, and they panic. Moses tries to calm them by praying to God for another miracle. God's response is unexpected but instructive:

> The Lord said to Moses, "Why do you cry to me? Tell the people of Israel to go forward. Lift up your staff, and stretch out your hand over the sea and divide it, that the people of Israel may go through the sea on dry ground. (Exodus 14:15–16 ESV)

In other words, God is saying, "This is not the time for prayer to me to rescue you. It is time for *you* to act, based on your faith in me."

Faith's Answers to America's Political Crisis

The later Midrashic elucidation of this section of Exodus by the rabbinical commentators adds a very meaningful element to the story. According to this Midrash, Moses held up his staff, as God had directed, but the waters of the Red Sea did not part. Then Nahshon, the head of the tribe of Judah, walked into the water to affirm his faith in God's miraculous promise to divide the sea. He moved farther and farther until the water was as high as his nostrils and he risked drowning. Then and only then did God divide the Red Sea, and the Israelites walked through to safety and freedom. Only after Nahshon's show of faith in God and the courage he displayed to take action did God separate the sea and save the Israelites from the pharaoh and his army.

That is exactly where we are metaphorically now in American politics. It is time for us to have faith and take courageous, corrective action. It is time for each of us to find the Nahshon inside ourselves. At similarly difficult and critical times in our history, the American people have been lifted up by religious awakenings that have moved them to act in ways that have made America a better and better country. Each of the awakenings, as the word suggests, followed times of relative slumber and led to extraordinary political, social, or cultural progress in America.

Historians generally agree that we have had four American religious awakenings. They began in 1735, 1805, 1865, and 1965. Each involved a return to religiosity, mostly among Christians, because Christianity historically has been the faith of most Americans—and still is the faith of two-thirds of Americans today, according to Pew Research Center. And each led to personal and communal activism for social justice and national or local progress.

Let's look first at the Great Awakening that occurred between 1720 and the 1740s. The intensity of Puritan spirituality in the colonies had faded since the end of the seventeenth century. The Great Awakening was a reaction to that, to the growing secularization of colonial American society, and to the leading American churches, which critics charged had become materialistic. Led by gifted clergymen like Jonathan Edwards and George Whitefield, the Great Awakening revived, evangelized, and democratized the Calvinist religious denominations in America. Those religious reforms in the established churches ushered in a new tolerance for religious diversity in America, and that in turn increased the popular support for the American Revolution and America's independence from England. In other words, the Great Awakening was actively present at the creation of the United States of America.

The second religious awakening (1840–1879) inspired single-issue Christian reform movements, each of which had the goal of improving the country and hastening the Second Coming of Jesus. These movements led to historic changes and events, including the abolitionist movement, the Civil War, the emancipation of the slaves, and the beginning of the campaign to allow women to vote.

Faith's Answers to America's Political Crisis

The third awakening (1890–1930) was focused on social "sins." It attacked business corruption and argued that poverty was not a personal failure but a national failure. As such, it should be reduced through governmental programs, including laws to protect working people and their conditions of labor and wages, along with progressive income taxes and continued advocacy for women's rights and civil rights.

The fourth awakening began around 1960 and focused on personal behavior. It was more "conservative"—pro-life and pro-family, supportive of traditional values in the media and in our culture, and of more value-oriented curricula in public schools. In many ways, this fourth awakening continues today.

Now we need a new religious awakening in America, whose goal is to bring the American people and their leaders back to bipartisan, problem-solving politics and government.

As was true before the other awakenings, the American people's religious affiliations have been declining. One of the premises of this book is that the great majority of the American people believe in God, but that they are not connecting that belief and the values that come from it to the political part of their lives as politicians or citizens. The number of Americans who believe in God remains high—81 percent, according to Gallup. But when we look at the religious affiliation of the American people, we see definite movement away from Christianity. In a survey done by the Pew Research

Center at the end of 2021, 63 percent of Americans identified themselves as Christian. That was 12 percent lower than it had been only ten years before. The Pew research shows that the people who left Christianity did not go to other religions; they just pulled away from religious affiliation in general. In the 2021 survey, about three in ten adults in the US (29 percent) chose "none" for their religion—atheism, agnosticism, or "nothing at all." Only fourteen years earlier, when Pew began asking the same question, only 16 percent had chosen "none"—13 percent fewer than in 2021.

A Gallup survey in 2021 showed that fewer than half of American adults belong to a church, synagogue, or mosque. That was the first time in the eighty years that Gallup had been asking that question that religious affiliation in America fell below 50 percent. In 1999, 70 percent had said they belonged to a religious congregation—an enormous change in little more than two decades. In a 2023 survey conducted for the *Wall Street Journal* by NORC, a research center at the University of Chicago, 39 percent of respondents said that religion was very important to them. This was a striking 23 percent lower than twenty-five years earlier, when the *Journal* had first asked the question.

That is the additional challenge religious leaders face now. They must mobilize the faithful to lift up and unite our politics and, at the same time, find a way to reengage with the many who have left their faith communities in the past couple of decades. I know that most of the American people—religiously affiliated or not—still believe in God and yearn for a better, more united way in our politics and government, and that should give confidence to our clergy in this mission. A spiritual road to such political reforms will not be taken automatically. It will take passionate and persistent outreach by clergy of all faiths to elected officials, to the people in the American media who have been fanning the flames of partisanship in their coverage of government and politics, and to all of the rest of us. It will require regular sermons from the pulpit teaching the connection between faith and faith-based values and the need for political reform. And it will take person-to-person spiritual engagement between clergy and their parishioners, including those who have stopped coming to services. The religious path to better politics and government in America will not be easy, but we know from the four previous religious awakenings that it can be done. It has been done. Four times in our history when America had big problems, leaders who were motivated by their faith brought about tremendous progress.

One of the most significant benefits of a new religious awakening in America is that it would reduce the pervasive and uncharacteristic pessimism about the future that now exists among the American people. There have been plenty of rapid changes in our economy, our population, our culture, and our environment that have certainly made people anxious about the future. But the failure of our political leaders to work together to solve the problems that have stemmed from these changes is deepening the dark mood of the public. Research consistently shows that religious people are more optimistic. That's why I believe a religious awakening would give more Americans the hope they need to get into the fight for political reform.

Not all the work to bring about a religious awakening can be done by clergy. Political leaders are one of the primary targets of the clergy, but they too can activate their faith and bring about the awakening. One way would be to come together across party lines and adopt a new American political covenant.

Covenants figure prominently in the Judeo-Christian and other religious traditions. They are mostly agreements between God and humans, in which each feels and pledges loyalty to the other, and both know good things will result from their agreement—their covenant. But covenants also can and must exist among people, and this is one of those times when America needs one.

In his book *The Dignity of Difference*, Chief Rabbi Jonathan Sacks eloquently defines what a covenant is, and the difference between that and a contract:

> Covenant is a bond, not of interest or advantage but of belonging. Covenants are made when two or more people come together to create a "We." They differ from contracts in that they tend to

be open-ended and enduring. They involve a substantive notion of loyalty—of staying together even in difficult times. They may call at times for self-sacrifice. People bound by a covenant are obligated to respond to one another beyond the letter of the law rather than to limit their obligations to the narrowest contractual requirements.

Then Rabbi Sacks added words that are directly relevant to America's current political crisis:

Covenantal relationships...where we develop the grammar and syntax of reciprocity...are where trust is born.... Contracts, social or economic, mediate relationships between strangers. But if we were always and only strangers to one another, we would have no reason to trust one another.... A world systematically bereft of fidelity [that is, trust] or loyalty would be one in which neither states nor markets would ever get under way.

Rabbi Sacks' words perfectly describe why we would benefit so much from a new American political covenant.

Senator Joe Lieberman

I want to recommend a formal coming together of our political leaders of all parties and ideologies, ideally at Independence Hall in Philadelphia, for the adoption of such a covenant, one that will reconnect us to the founding values and spirit that were expressed in that hall in the Declaration of Independence and the Constitution—both grand covenantal agreements. Could there be a greater inspiration for a new American political covenant and a new religious awakening than the final words of the Declaration?

> And for the support of this Declaration,
> with a firm reliance on the protection of
> Divine Providence, we mutually pledge
> to each other our lives, our fortunes, and
> our sacred honor.

That is the high ground of national interest our political leaders need to return to in a new covenantal declaration. Once there, they can decry the loss of trust and reciprocity among them and the rest of us, and call for a new covenant. This covenant would establish the national goal of bringing us badly divided Americans—"I's"—back together to create a "We," as in "We the people of the United States"—the words that begin the Constitution.

I hope such a covenant would declare that the "We" would be based on our faith that we are all children of the same God, as we are of Abraham, with whom God made a great and lasting covenant, and based on the political reality that we are all free citizens of the same great country with a wonderful shared history—and, if we can protect and revive that history, an even better shared future. I believe that such a nonpartisan statement of national revival and purpose would lead to countless acts by our leaders and us citizens to restore our national unity, cleanse our politics, and rebuild our government.

Can we do it? That is now up to us, as it was up to Nahshon of the tribe of Judah at the Red Sea.

As President Kennedy said in his Inaugural Address, which moved so many of my generation into a covenant for public service:

> With a good conscience our only sure reward, with history as the final judge of our deeds, let us go forth to lead the land we love, asking His blessing and His help, but knowing that here on earth God's work must truly be our own.